EURIG SCANDRETT job shares the post of Head of Community Action at Friends of the Earth Scotland and teaches environmental policy with the Open University. He is on the National Council of Democratic Left Scotland.

SARAH BOYACK MSP represents Edinburgh Central in the Scottish Parliament. Formerly a lecturer in planning at Heriot Watt University, she was the Scottish Executive's first Minister for Transport and the Environment.

MARK BALLARD is the Secretary of the Council of the Scottish Green Party and a former editor of the *Reforesting Scotland* Journal and *Climax*, the magazine of the International Youth Climate Campaign.

STUART DUFFIN is Chief Executive of West Lothian Chamber of Commerce and of the Avon Chamber of Commerce and Innovation. He is the Chair of AGENDA: Social Responsibility in Scotland; Treasurer of West Lothian Youth Theatre; Chair of the Central Board of Young Enterprise Scotland; and a Board Member of Community Enterprise Limited. He was formerly Director of the Citizen's Income Study Centre of the London School of Economics

BARBARA MACLENNAN is a member of the International Association for Feminist Economics. She has taught economics at the universities of York and Manchester and convened a series of interdisciplinary gender seminars at the European University Institute in Italy.

OSBERT LANCASTER is Executive Director of the Centre for Human Ecology, Scotland's alternative university for ecology and community, and previously led CHE's work on business and sustainability. He has worked as a manager in the private sector; as a management consultant in Scotland and Eastern Europe; and as a business development adviser with small and medium sized enterprises.

RICHARD LEONARD was formerly economist at the STUC, and is now political officer and industrial organiser at the GMB. He is currently Chairperson of the Scottish Labour Party.

MARY SPOWART has been an independent and parliamentary researcher since 1996 specialising in environmental policy. She has worked in environmental NGOs in Scotland and Kenya and is a member of Democratic Left Scotland.

Scotlands of the Future
Sustainability in a small nation

Introduced and edited by
EURIG SCANDRETT

Luath Press Limited
EDINBURGH
www.luath.co.uk

Published in association with

democratic left scotland

Democratic Left Scotland is a non-party political organization working for progressive social change through activity in civil society – in community groups, social movements and single-issue campaigns. DLS seeks to promote discussion and alliances across the lines of party, position and identity from a standpoint that is radical, feminist and green. Further information is available from:

Democratic Left Scotland
1A Leopold Place
Edinburgh EH7 5JW
Tel: 0131 477 2997
E-mail: dls@newpolitics.org.uk
Web: www.newpolitics.org.uk

Democratic Left Scotland is grateful to the Barry Amiel and Norman Melburn Trust for financial support for this publication. Many thanks to the contributors, and to Stuart Fairweather, David Purdy and particularly to Jane Corrie for their support for the project.

First Published 2003

The paper used in this book is acid-free, neutral-sized and recyclable. It is made from low chlorine pulps produced in a low energy, low emission manner from sustainable forests.

Printed and bound by
Bell and Bain Ltd., Glasgow

Typeset in Sabon 10.5 by Sarah Crozier, Nantes

Contents

Introduction

Towards a new agenda for a sustainable economy in Scotland

EURIG SCANDRETT

Scotland is unsustainable. We continue to suffer from the scandals of inequality and environmental damage – at home, globally and between generations.

Within Scotland, as in all nations, environmental damage is unevenly distributed, with the most degraded and dangerous environments closest to people who are poor, geographically isolated, socially marginalised and politically disenfranchised. Globally, Scotland is part of the so called 'developed world', the former colonisers, who unjustly impact on the majority population of the world who are living in poverty. And our over-consumption of the world's natural resources leaves an unpaid historical legacy on the world, and depletes the quality of life of future generations.

We need to move towards sustainability. In a sustainable Scotland, the treatment of society and the natural resources on which that society depends, promotes a good quality of life for our own and future generations.

Any transition to a sustainable society must be well grounded in economics. Economics describes the ways in which natural, human and manufactured resources are transformed into social goods and distributed amongst those who use them. Economics also interprets the distribution of the damage caused by this production and consumption, and shapes the limitations and the opportunities for social relations.

All the authors of this volume are actively engaged in

promoting social change towards a sustainable economy in Scotland through their participation in civil society and democratic politics. Progressive thinking on sustainable economics is one of the most creative areas of development worldwide, involving theorists and activists in socialist, libertarian and green traditions. It draws on the various experiments with community- and worker-led economic change and sets this in the context of challenging the global maldistribution and the absolute limitations of natural resources. The articles produced here are therefore partial. None of the authors is currently a full time professional academic (although several have recently been so) and the publication is not intended to be academic, nor to rival the important work which some academics are doing in the field of sustainability economics.

Scotland's changing context

Scotland is in a unique position. The relationship between its ecological and economic base, its democratic politics and its civil society is shifting. This provides an opportunity for exploring and intervening in social change with long term implications.

The Scottish Parliament, more than any other devolved assembly in the United Kingdom, was the product of civil society. In the 1990s, whilst Scotland voted increasingly for non-Tory parties and experienced successive Tory victories in the UK, various civil society organisations worked together with political parties under the banner of the Scottish Constitutional Convention. With the Labour victory in 1997, the Convention paved the way for the structure of the parliament which was installed in 1998. Prominent individuals from within civil society were appointed to the Consultative Steering Group, which proposed the methods of operation of the Scottish Parliament, to encourage openness and accountability.

In the first elections, the proportional representation electoral system delivered a completely new political formation for the UK: a centre-left coalition Executive, Nationalist opposition and a small Tory group. Representation was also achieved for Socialist and Green Parties and Denis Canavan as a (socialist) independent. A robust committee structure has strengthened the Parliament relative to the Executive. In addition, significant parts of civil society formed the Scottish Civic Assembly as early as 1995, and this body lobbied for and eventually was succeeded by the Scottish Civic Forum, with non-statutory responsibilities to facilitate access between civil society and the Parliament and its Executive.

Despite devolution of most environmental and social responsibilities, major economic decisions are still made outwith Scotland. Macro-economic policy remains the reserve of Westminster. Centripetal economic trends within the European bloc tend to peripheralise Scotland's economy to servicing growth elsewhere with cheap labour and primary resources. Internationally, World Trade Organisation rules and the continuing orthodoxy of trade liberalisation put economic decision-making beyond the control of any democratic institution.

As the discussions in this volume demonstrate, however, agency for change in Scotland is strong. There are significant opportunities for long term economic change for sustainability, democracy and social justice, which can harness the political energy in parliament and civil society to make real changes for a sustainable economy.

The purpose of this publication is therefore both analytical and practical, to provide a platform for activists to reflect critically on the process of moving to a sustainable economy in Scotland, and also to stimulate the political action which will make it a reality. Moreover, the process of producing the book has attempted to embody this. As analytical activists, the authors contributed a draft of their ideas to a seminar in April 2002. This seminar gave people the opportunity to present ideas, including those which were untested, and receive constructive critical feedback. Having been through this process, the articles were worked up in the following months to reach their present form. This writing has been done largely in the authors' own time as they have continued to be active in the organisations, unions and parties which gives them the experience from which to reflect. I am grateful therefore for their time and energies.

There is a complex and dialectical relationship between ecology, the economy, civil society, the state, ideas, political action and critical analysis. It is hoped that using the method described above has led to a publication which is useful to those who are engaged in building a sustainable economy.

Economic discussions on the left have often focused on questions of the relationship between the economy and politics. Sections of the left are tied to an economic determinism that has scarcely engaged with the economy of ecology. In some cases this tradition has also resisted engagement with politics at the level of the devolved parliament. According to this narrative, global economic forces are concentrating economic power in the hands of progressively fewer multinationals whose power over elected governments is increasing. Even nation states are seeking to negotiate away their power of accountability through successive international agreements – the General Agreement on Tariffs and Trade (GATT) and its successor World Trade Organisation (WTO), the failed Multilateral Agreement on Investment (MAI) and its replacement General Agreement on Trade in Services (GATS). For advocates of this narrative, engagement in government is futile and it is through revolutionary control of the economy that progress can be made. The anti-globalisation movement and Social Forums in Porto Alegre and Florence are providing leadership to these changes.

On the other hand, the mainstream left has largely given up on transforming the economy. The purpose of the Blairite project and also of a sector of green thought is to allow the market economy a free run with only minor nudging in the direction of socialising (or ecologising) it. The economy is too big and complex to be controlled by politics, and works better without political interference. Let those who understand the market economy do what they do best: the powerful business sector, the Bank of England, the European Central Bank. The purpose of (left) politics from this perspective therefore is to ensure that everyone has a fair access to this liberated and growing economy as worker, producer, entrepreneur, investor, consumer and service user. The economic role of the state is to coax or cajole people into the market economy, and to tinker with the parameters where market failures are likely to be unacceptable.

In the environmental arena this is influenced, where at all, by European ecological modernisation: regulation is for the last resort, the market is the engine of ecological protection if you can just align the interests of capital with those of the environment. Market tinkering by way of resource taxes and trading in environmental goods and costs is regarded as the way to create a sustainable economy by such orthodoxy. The problem with the market economy (by this account) is not that it is inadequately constrained but that it is too constrained, and the more we can incorporate the 'external' environmental impact into market forces, the more the market will act to value the goods and minimise the costs.

This publication arises from the belief that neither revolutionary nor 'third-way' economic determinism is adequate. It is true that an understanding of the economic structure underlying class (and other) power distribution is essential. Attempts to manage everything and abolish markets are also highly suspect. However, a sustainable economy will not simply be a tinkered-with market, but neither will it wait for a spontaneous revolution. Positive political engagement is possible.

Moreover, neither of these (admittedly caricatured) economic analyses adequately recognises the dependence of the economy on ecology – on the natural resources, the energy, the sinks for waste disposal and the life-support cycles of the Earth's ecosystem. Even a supposedly post-industrial, knowledge-based economy such as Scotland's betrays its material dependence in local conflicts over living environments, in the coal-fields and quarry sites, the fishing communities, fish farms, waste landfills and incinerators. The apparently dematerialising economy simply exports its dirty processes to poorer and newly developing countries and continues to jeopardise the global climate by its oil dependence.

So it is in the interaction between ecology and economy; between politics and economics; between state and civil society; between the local and the global; and between social movements and democratic policy making; that movement to a sustainable society for Scotland will occur. This is the space where these articles engage.

Opportunities from civil society

The authors of this publication are all reflective practitioners in the politics of civil society with a strong appreciation of and commitment to building a sustainable economy. By virtue of their practical engagement, none of these articles is utopian and the book gives no blueprint for a sustainable economy for Scotland. They are all, however, visionary. The task set for the authors was to write of the future whilst keeping their feet firmly in the reality of practical politics, whether it be trade union negotiating, NGO campaigning, media polemic, stimulating business development or organising in communities. There is an important epistemology in this. We will not know how to move forward by pretending that we are somehow 'above' the reality of the existing economic and political struggles, untouched by the messiness of engagement. In Marx's familiar words, whilst philosophers interpret the world in different ways, the point is to change it. Neither abstract theorising nor mindless activism alone will give us much indication of the way forward, but rather reflection, collectively within and amongst our social movements and organisations. It is hoped that this publication will be a contribution to such praxis (figure 1.1).

Whilst this book does not set out to define where we aim to get to, it does identify how we are getting there. The shape of the sustainable economy is emerging from the diverse struggles in Scotland. We will not define what a sustainable economy is (indeed the authors may disagree on this) but we know what it will be like. Themes which arise in the publication are perhaps not surprising, but it is worth emphasising particularly those

Figure 1.1
The praxis of change towards a
sustainable economy

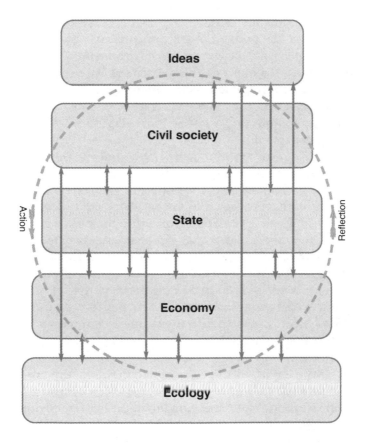

issues which are neglected in the mainstream discourse on sustainable economics. Thus we can say that a sustainable economy is accountable and democratic; it focuses on the level of society with which people most engage; it gives a priority to those who are currently disenfranchised by the social and ecological outcomes of economic processes; it works with rather than against the ecology in which it is set; and it takes full consideration of the global and intergenerational context.

To be sustainable, Scotland's economy therefore must be accountable to the needs of people, in particular the needs of the most vulnerable and the victims of environmental injustices, to communities, to women, to those excluded from power, and in the last instance accountable to the ultimate limitations which the ecology of the Earth puts upon us. This is both an accountability to future generations and a respect for a natural world which we still dimly understand.

This book looks to embrace the potential for this change. It starts with the opportunities of the new parliament, the conversion of Labour and the influence of the environmental movement both through the Green Party and through civil society. It looks at the opportunities for making the economy work for those who currently lose out, the unemployed and underemployed, and those whose work is not recognised despite it being at the forefront of building a socially and environmentally sustainable economy. It addresses the problem that most of these victims live outwith Scotland in the poorest countries and economies, and looks at how we value the things which are important. Finally, it looks at new opportunities for building a sustainable economy in Scotland, both in policy terms and in the practice of people's lives, work, families, communities and political action.

Sarah Boyack, is in the unique position of having been Scotland's first ever Environment Minister, yet at the time of writing enjoys the relative independence of the back benches. She argues that much has been achieved for a sustainable economy in Scotland's first Parliament. Whilst advocating for Labour's role in leading the Executive coalition, she also argues that the successes have been achieved in a large part due to the open and accountable structure of the Parliament, the changing support and participation of Labour party members, and the effectiveness and responsibility of NGOs and others in civil society. Reactionary pressures are continually experienced, not least from a media with a superficial understanding of the issues of democracy and sustainability. There is clearly a vast gap between where we are and where we could be on the road to a sustainable economy. However, Boyack argues that the fact that there have been advances illustrates a shift in the relationship between the state and civil society in Scotland. Does this offer a glimpse of the 'educated and participating democracy' envisioned by the cultural critic Raymond Williams? It can certainly provide a motivation for those in civil society who are actively working for a sustainable Scotland.

Mark Ballard brings tremendous experience from the perspective of the environmental press and NGOs and of the Scottish Green Party. Possibly more than any other party, the Greens have emerged from the 'new social movements' and pride themselves on retaining the culture and connections with the sector. Whilst Ballard's article is not a Green Party document, it reflects the way in which the party and the green movement has developed together. Ballard emphasises the growth of community enterprise and especially that which relates to a significant natural resource in Scotland, the forests. If the economy is to be sustainable it must be tackled at both ends, stimulating ecologically rooted community enterprise at the bottom, and at the top, re-orientating the fiscal strategy towards socially and environmentally just ends.

The fiscal system is also the concern of **Stuart Duffin**, not just as a means of redistributing resources but of liberating people. Taxation has been turned into a political bogeyman and few political leaders are willing to show any lead on the potential for sustainable taxation. On the other hand, benefits are regarded as no more than safety nets, an admission of failure where those who are 'economically unproductive' may at least receive a basic standard of living. The idea of a citizens' income continues to provide a radical alternative, the proposal that all citizens should have a right to an income independent of employment or means. Duffin demonstrates how integrating the taxation and benefits systems into a citizens' income is good for business, good for the unemployed and under-employed, good for the economy as a whole and makes for a more sustainable community.

Barbara MacLennan focuses on the household and community sectors of the economy. Whilst women are systematically excluded from economic power in the business and public sectors, they make many economic decisions which affect the quality of life of communities. MacLennan applies a feminist analysis to time and money and proposes practical reforms which would shift the balance of power to women and their communities. In particular, a simple reform in banking regulation to promote community reinvestment would transform the nature of the economy, by encouraging a reassessment of what is valued.

Problems with the way goods are currently valued in the economy is the point where **Osbert Lancaster** begins his critique. The existing global orthodoxy of economic liberalisation is not only flawed but exposed as no more than a bias to the rich. Lancaster reminds us of the ways in which our standard of living is maintained at the expense of the poor in the poorest countries, and how we do not pay for the social and environmental damage which we cause. Whilst there are attempts to include such costs into economic transactions, Lancaster assesses the limitations of this endeavour and looks at ways in which Scotland's economy could express values other than those which can be measured in financial terms. Existing initiatives, such as fair trade, provide the pointers to the way forward. Whilst action is clearly needed at international level, much can be done domestically to ensure that a vibrant business sector does not exploit people and planet.

Finally, **Richard Leonard** makes the case for a 'just transition' to sustainability in Scotland. The importance of trades unions in building sustainable development was recognised in 1992 in Agenda 21: '...trade unions are vital actors in facilitating the achievement of sustainable development in view of their experience in addressing industrial change, the extremely high priority they give to protection of the working environment and the related natural environment and their promotion of socially responsible and economic development' (Quarrie 1992). This has seldom been realised, although Leonard's union, the GMB, has made significant progress recently. As Leonard points out, the transition to a sustainable economy not only requires the participation of organised workers if it is to be a 'just transition', but also the skills and experience of Scottish workers can be an asset to sustainability. Whether it be transforming the oil fabrication yards, diversifying defence industries or developing co-operatives, workers' skills and organisation are essential to a sustainable economy. Thus, Scotland is in an excellent position industrially as well as ecologically, to be a green enterprise centre for Europe.

As editor of this collection, I inevitably draw on my experience at Friends of the Earth (FOE) Scotland. Friends of the Earth has been one of the foremost environmental NGOs active in Scotland addressing issues of sustainable development and environmental justice, although to date the economy has largely escaped the direct focus of its gaze. However, there are areas of FOE's work which distinctively tackle the political ecology of conflicts over environmental costs and benefits. FOE Scotland has focused much of its work in recent years on supporting local communities engaged in conflicts over environmental damage. Also internationally, Friends of the Earth has grappled with the question of ecological limitations through the calculation of the environmental space. Combining these two – local community struggle with the ecological limitations – has led to a campaign priority of environmental justice for Scotland as 'no less than a decent environment for all, with no more than our fair share of the Earth's resources'.

The publication is completed with an assessment, by **Mary Spowart**, of the more practical political implications of the arguments of the other chapters. Some of what the contributors have advocated would require legislation, whether at Holyrood, Westminster or Brussels, and the legislative changes may be achievable in short term political reality, or else require a process of persuasion and alliance building for more significant change in the future. Other areas of change involve policy or practice in local government or civil society, or in the quasi autonomous regulatory or enterprise agencies. Teasing out these implications, Spowart has provided 'toolkit for activists', a list of the most significant changes advocated by these authors for a sustainable Scotland, arranged according to their political opportunity and augmented by a website. This is clearly not a manifesto: it makes no claim to be exhaustive, priorities will vary amongst groups, and some objectives may be contradictory. However, it is hoped that this list and website will help the book to be of more direct use to Scotland's citizens lobbying and campaigning for a sustainable economy.

A political economy of Scotland

The economy of Scotland, as everywhere, relies on the extraction or harvesting, manufacture, distribution, consumption and ultimate disposal of materials; harnessing, transforming and dissipating energy in the process. Each of these processes happen somewhere and affects the communities that live there. There are people who live beside the farms and fish farms, the quarries and mines, the power stations and factories, the roads and airports, the landfill sites and incinerators (figure 1.2). Moreover, the processes of economic decision-making lead to the most damaging of these developments to be positioned beside the poorest, the disenfranchised, the geographically isolated, those with the least power. In the economy of the marketplace, the poor sell cheap – their land, their labour, their health, their environment, all come cheaper than those with economic and political power.

Similarly, in the market for the benefits of the economy, the goods and services which these resources and energy produce, it

Figure 1.2
Environmental injustices
caused by resource flows

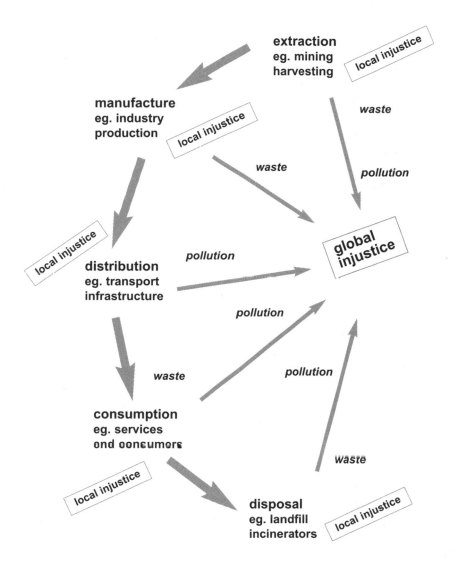

is the poor again who lose out, who do not have access to the goods and services. The ecologically and economically poor, therefore have poor quality housing and least choice of foods, they live beside busy roads but have no access to a car, they are in isolated towns whilst the services move to the city, they consume few luxuries but live with the waste of a profligate society, they live beside the quarry but see little construction from which they will benefit.

Fortunately, people in such circumstances resist. They organise and campaign against the developments the impacts of which they suffer, but from which they will not benefit. Many of these activists would not describe themselves as environmentalists. However, these communities of resistance are at the forefront of the sustainable economy, because they take action at the point where the unsustainable economy bites, the conflict over the distribution of environmental costs, benefits and resources. This is where the future meets the present – our continual insistence on living on far more than the Earth can supply means that these conflicts over environmental resources will become increasingly common and desperate.

The green economic argument is that society should be living off the interest of the Earth's capital, rather than depleting the capital stocks themselves. This is sound but appears impractical given the extent of exploitation which we currently rely on. How do we get from our current excessive and unsustainable ecological exploitation, to living within our means, without the complete devastation of the lives of the poorest in the world? The model of the environmental space has been used by Friends of the Earth groups throughout the world to seek a solution to this.

Environmental Space is one of the indicators of impact on the earth (along with ecological footprint or rucksack). Originating in the work of the Wuppertal Institute in Germany, environmental space involves a calculation for the rate of use of each of the Earth's resources without breaching its most limiting environmental factor. These limiting factors include the stock of the resource which can be exploited without causing local damage, and the capacity of ecological processes to absorb the waste stream generated by use of the resource. The total rate at which each resource can therefore be exploited without causing irreparable damage to the ecosystem, is then shared amongst the population which has legitimate right to access this resource (which in most cases is the global population). Thus, a ure for the environmental space for each resource may be theoretically calculated, and expressed in a rate of use per capita per year (figure 1.3).

Figure 1.3
The environmental space

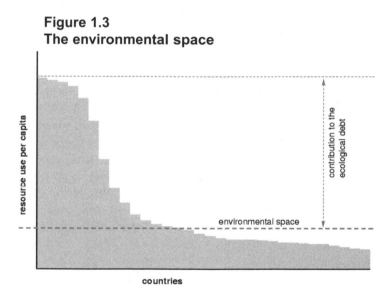

For virtually all resources calculated, the North uses more than its environmental space. However, if we are able to reduce our resource use to that of the environmental space level then we will have achieved both global equity (because the rich countries will not use more than our fair share of the earth's resources, enabling the poorer countries to use resources for their own development) and intergenerational equity (because our resource use will not leave future generations with an irreparably damaged environment). However, if we do not achieve environmental space levels, we will be continuing to exploit both the rest of the world and future generations. Sharing the environmental space means living within our means.

When applied to Scotland, a majority of the resources for which calculations have been made require a reduction in our use of between 80 and 90%. This is a tough target, but it has been estimated that this is possible to achieve over a period of about two generations if the appropriate mechanisms are in place (FOE Scotland 1996). If these are the targets and this the timescale, the tasks for political action towards a sustainable economy start to take shape.

Some economists argue that exploiting today's ecology is justified by the capital which is generated and therefore inherited by future generations – financial capital is substitutable for ecological capital. The theoretical flaws in this argument are beyond the scope of this publication, although the maldistribution of ownership of the capital, and the problems of attaching a value to ecological resources, present themselves daily in the practice of economic decision making. However, in the short term, we may have no choice but to use the capital of past exploitation to invest in a future sustainable economy.

The problem is, it is the 'developed' economies of the North which have benefited from the capital extracted from the ecologies of the 'developing' economies of the South. Indeed, the strongest criticism of environmental space is that it sets a target of equal per capita resource use without taking cognisance of the historical legacy and ongoing exploitation of the ecologies of the North and the South, and of the global commons. A situation in which we achieve a fair distribution of resource use will institute a global inequality derived from the wealth which the North has accumulated on the back of centuries of resource exploitation. The North has accumulated an ecological debt, which must be paid in some form in order to achieve equality. Putting this another way, reparations are due to the countries of the South for the long history and continuation of their exploitation (figure 1.4).

How a country such as Scotland can repay its ecological debt is a subject which needs to be addressed. In addition to reducing our resource use to at least the level of the environmental space,

Figure 1.4
Accumulation of ecological debt

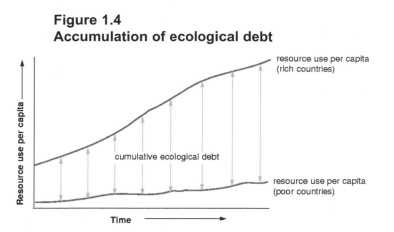

there are other global obligations to fulfil. In theory, this could take the form of cancellation of the South's external debts, financial and technological transfers or relaxing of immigration barriers from the South. The details and practice of repaying the ecological debt are still far from the reality of politics, but the value of these insights is to shift the focus of the political discourse. It is morally inadequate to discuss attaching political conditions for debt remission to the poorest indebted nations unless equivalent conditions are attached to our own, ecologically indebted country. Aid and technology transfer must be discussed as a debtor's duty, or the penance of a thief, not the philanthropy of an altruistic civilisation, nor a business opportunity. The politically volatile discussions about immigration need an injection of humility. The question of how to keep people out should be countered with a demand for justification for denying anyone access to the ecological wealth which we have plundered.

Taken together, the two facets of environmental justice – a decent environment for all with no more than our share (excluding or including our ecological debt) of the Earth's resources – focus attention on the land use planning system, an issue not addressed by the current authors. Scotland's land use planning system, by comparison with some such systems in the world, is not bad, but some fundamental flaws in the way in which it operates lead to environmental injustices. The system is a means of submitting the use of land to some degree of democratic control, and of balancing the competing claims of individuals, communities and society. It rightly separates the financial cost-benefit analysis of development companies from the specific non-financial quality of life claims of those who will be affected, guided in the process by nationally agreed policy. With the exception of small but significant anomalies (such as the lack of third party rights of appeal, and the specific cases of local authority developments), all developers are treated equitably in theory, as are all third parties, and checks and balances are in place to protect this.

Nevertheless it is naïve to expect a system which is designed on equitable access to produce an equal outcome. Powerful groups such as development companies and significant landowners have greater capacity to lobby in the formation of plans and guidance and in the submission of specific development proposals, and to defend their interests with legal and administrative resources in the case of disputes. Despite references to sustainable development, there is an ideological assumption that virtually all development is in the public interest, that it should go ahead unless there are compelling reasons not to, thus shifting the burden of proof on the objectors. Moreover, in a dominant market based system based on cheap (effectively subsidised) private transport costs, the planning system largely does no more than predict and provide, placing some constraints on free development and at best coaxing the market to provide the kind of developments desired. This is considerably better than having no planning system, but the opportunities for integrating landuse planning with other planning functions of local and national government, including economic planning, is enormous.

Development planning is not addressed in this book, and neither is that other important area of conflict over resources, land reform. Land reform was the subject of another recent collaboration between Democratic Left Scotland and Luath Press. In *Scotland, Land and Power*, Andy Wightman argues that recent legislation has brought Scottish land tenure systems into the twentieth century, but no further. Real land reform, in which power over land is redistributed, still has some way to go. However, it is starting, in some of the most peripheral areas of Scotland's crofting lands. This revolution now needs to spread, not only to all of Scotland's rural and urban land, but also to all of our natural resources and, as Richard Leonard argues, to our industries too. Scottish devolution is but one, significant step in the direction of a wholesale democratisation of our political and ecological economy.

Devolution in Scotland, a small country on the edge of Europe, has increased the potential for making progress towards a sustainable economy. Indeed, with some visionary political leadership in government and in civil society, the country could take a lead in such developments. Scotland's history contains a rich heritage of contributions to sustainability. Patrick Geddes initiated regional planning on socio-ecological grounds and promoted balanced development through the progression of 'work, folk and place' (which resonates with the 'economy, society and environment' of more recent sustainability literature). A little later, Frank Fraser Darling's studies of the North Western Highlands made a significant contribution to founding the discipline of human ecology. Earlier, John Muir left Scotland and became the founder of the American wilderness movement, emphasising the non-instrumental values of nature. Even going back to the 13th Century, the theology of John Duns Scotus challenged, from what some have described as an ecological perspective, Thomas Aquinas' emphasis on humanity-nature dualism.

Many others, whose names have less immortality, have worked to bring about a sustainable economy, whether through the workplace and trade union, or the family and the community, whether through resistance to the bad or through stimulating the good. The contributors to this book are participants in such a project. Their chapters demonstrate their praxis – their combinations of action and reflection – which will be necessary to build a sustainable economy. To be sustainable, Scotland's economy must be built on praxis. It must arise out of a reflection on action and acting out of reflecting together. Democratic Left Scotland is privileged to have hosted this opportunity for these contributors to reflect together. We hope that those reading it will be encouraged to act.

References

FoE Scotland (1996), *Towards a Sustainable Scotland*, Friends of the Earth, Edinburgh.
Quarrie, J, (ed.) (1992), *Earth Summit 1992*, The Regency Press, London
Wightman, A (1999) *Scotland, Land and Power: the agenda for land reform*, Luath Press, Edinburgh

2

A lot done: a lot still to do?

Environmental achievements in the first term of the Scottish Parliament and challenges for the second

SARAH BOYACK

Thinking ahead to the second term of the Scottish Parliamentary session, it is worth drawing on the lessons of the first term. This contribution does not aim to be encyclopaedic: a comprehensive analysis could justify a book in itself. But I want to question how far we've delivered on the aims and ambitions that we saw that could be delivered by a Labour led Scottish Executive. That would set a path for the next term. What should be our ambitions second time around?

Aspirations for the Parliament

As a long-standing campaigner in the Labour Party for a more meaningful engagement with environmental challenges, my principal ambition in the run up to devolution was that we pushed consideration of the environment up the political agenda.

For me that meant a more joined-up approach to politics. That meant not seeing the environment as an add-on extra once our other priorities have been met. Our policies on economic prosperity could make the most of the opportunities that a greener economic strategy could deliver for Scotland. We could make the crucial link between social justice and the environment. That meant, for example, delivering housing and social policies that made explicit the links between fuel poverty and energy efficiency.

Before the Parliament was established one of my fervent hopes was that there would be greater political interest in environmental issues, with better accountability and the scope for action and leadership on the key challenges facing us. That would mean regular debates that addressed environmental concerns in the Parliament, debates that would hold Ministers and the Executive to account.

Labour's rediscovery of environmental issues

On policy issues we found major challenges. Labour's manifesto for the first term set out ambitions which were consistent with our objectives to improve people's quality of life, tackle poverty, and to attack the scourge of unemployment by modernising our economy and regenerating our communities.

Our environmental commitments were significant. They reflected the hard lobbying in the party by SERA (Labour's environment campaign) and a battle of ideas. The last decade has seen extensive dialogue with Labour and environmentalists both in Scotland and at UK level. For us in the Labour Party the priority has been trying to reconnect environmental issues with our historic aspirations for improving people's quality of life and seeing action on sustainable development as a way to achieve that aspiration.

In a pamphlet on *Environmental Modernisation: The New Labour Agenda* (1999) Michael Jacob, the Fabians' General Secretary, commented that the perception that the environment is owned by the Greens and the environment NGOS (Non Governmental Organisations) prevents it from being embraced by the Labour Party. The role of trade unions in focusing on our environmental aspirations has also been important, for example in raising awareness on the potential benefits that renewable energy could bring to Scottish manufacturing. Environmental modernisation was linked to job creation.

For us in the Labour Party, we have travelled a very long way in a short space of time. If we go back to our roots as a party we've always been concerned with people's working and living environment. It has driven the party and trade union movement since our early days. But I would argue that it has only been in the last decade – since the Rio Conference – that we've linked our commitment to the environment directly with our economic ambitions.

Recapturing the environmental debate and bringing some commitment and ownership to Labour Party members has been one of the achievements of the first term of the Scottish Parliament.

Labour's first manifesto for the Scottish Parliament

The manifesto for the 1999 Scottish Parliament election focused on the importance of sustainable development. It also defined it as integrating 'the maintenance and enhancement of our natural and historic environment and the promotion of new opportunities for social and economic development in urban and rural areas'.

The manifesto highlighted the new policy direction set in Labour's first two years of government since 1997 as:

- taking action on 'greening government' in every government department; accelerating the renewable energy programme;
- taking comprehensive action to improve air quality and reduce the pollution generated by road traffic;
- reviewing planning policy on open-cast mines reviewing SEPA's (Scottish Environment Protection Agency) powers and increased resources;
- making water authorities more accountable;
- promoting energy efficiency through the Warm Deal.
- new commitments were also made to set up National Parks, revision of SSSIs (Sites of Special Scientific Interest) and giving a new direction to SNH (Scottish Natural Heritage).

A culture change in the Parliament

There is much to be positive about in relation to the environment and sustainable development in the Parliament. On a whole range of issues important progress is being made and there is far greater transparency and partnership in the process of delivery. But there is still much more to do.

Our political culture is still very tentative and sometimes dismissive when it comes to dealing with the environment. It also rewards short-termism and which can kick longer term difficult thinking into touch. Moreover, if the EU requires legislation then it overrides other priorities and is pushed up the list (although EU legislation often sets new environmental requirements).

In an article in 1999 I argued that key challenges would be:

- modernising our planning system and making it more effective;
- re-establishing regional and strategic planning – particularly across the central belt;
- making decisions on transport investment allied to strategic priorities; and
- redressing the historic imbalance left by the Conservatives where in the year before Labour was elected in 1997 not one penny was spent on capital investment in public transport.

The issue of the urban environment was also high on my agenda.

Historically the environment in Scotland has been seen as high quality, but this has more to do with a romantic view of our hills and ignores the reality of life in urban Scotland. It overlooks the problems caused by traffic congestion, open cast coal mining and the impact of decades of unsustainable waste management.

A key challenge for the new government in Scotland was that there was so much to do and such high expectations. This made the task of setting priorities vital. But with such an ambitious agenda across the whole of government it was never going to be possible to please everyone – never mind in the first four years. Yet it's not a story which has been told before.

The civil service was gearing up from Labour's first two years in power at Westminster to deliver on national parks and energy efficiency.

But the exciting story of the first term of the Parliament has been how much further we have been able to go than we promised. Attempting to come to terms with Scotland's contribution to meeting UK climate change objectives and making the most of our natural assets in an environmentally sustainable way has required taking a pragmatic approach to translating radical challenges into practical political action.

It is important that we log achievement and do not just focus on bad news stories. Do people know how much has been achieved? This is vital in connecting people to the political decision making process. Those who have engaged in the dialogue locally, in NGOs, or with the Parliament's Committees will have some understanding. It is important as our new democracy in Scotland begins to make a difference, as one of the four founding principles of the Scottish Parliament was access and consultation to decision making.

No news is good news

Dealing with the media is a major challenge on the environment – firstly making the case to the relevant news editor that it is a real story and then hoping that a journalist will understand the significance of the issue. With a very few honourable exceptions this is rarely the case.

I remember having a rather delicate conversation with Kevin Dunion, then Chief Executive of Friends of the Earth Scotland, about the need for some acknowledgement of progress being made by government. He observed that a recent Friends of the Earth press release had spent 90% of its length acknowledging and welcoming new action. It concluded with a highly reasonable comment at the end focusing on how much further we needed to go. The following press coverage however all led with an interpretation that Friends of the Earth had slammed the Executive.

Alternatively there might be simply no coverage at all!

A lot done, a lot still to do

'A lot done – a lot still to do' was Labour's slogan for the Scottish Parliament Elections in May 1999. It could serve as a useful judgement for the Scottish Executive's progress so far on the environment. There has been some significant progress on issues such as housing, renewable energy, planning and transport, but more limited progress on waste, agriculture and economic development.

Transport

For the first time in a generation, transport investment is at the heart of the political agenda. There has been a historic shift in resources. The transport budget is now spent with a much greater focus on public transport, walking and cycling.

In 1996/7, 12% of the Scottish transport budget went on public transport. By 2003, 53% will be spent on public transport and this includes a 45% increase in Scottish Executive spending on transport generally from 1999 levels. This represents a genuine political and cultural shift.

Inheriting twenty major road schemes from the outgoing Tory Government presented a major challenge. Labour made a commitment to review them against wider transport, environmental, safety and economic objectives. However there was not a comparable list of projects to assess or the framework to consider what was possible or desirable in relation to strategic rail or bus investment.

The multi-modal studies initiated after the Strategic Roads Review in 1999, which finally reported in January 2003, set the framework for an integrated approach to strategic and balanced transport investment. Allied to the Central Scotland Railway Capacity Study and the Airports Study these reports lay the framework for massive future investment. Setting priorities and a combination of public and private investment will especially be needed in rail projects given the range of players and the escalation of costs.

In the City of Edinburgh, investment by the Scottish Executive into tram options and discussions on the use of powers under the Transport Scotland 2001 Act open up the potential of a new network of trams across the city and dedicated transport investment in the city for the long term.

But crucially some of the most important investment in transport is not just the big projects, but sustained investment into buses, walking and cycling.

There are now many new projects coming on stream with signs of the first increase in bus use in decades. Where there has been concerted investment in buses with new, more attractive low-floor vehicles, better timetabling and more frequent services along dedicated bus lanes, people will and do use buses.

Ideas such as Home Zones, Safer Routes to School and investment in cycle ways and traffic calming can make a difference in encouraging safety people to think about positive alternatives to the car.

Planning guidelines have progressively required public transport access in new developments and reduced the requirement for car parking spaces. But there remains the challenge of de-coupling the assumption that more and bigger roads are inextricably linked to economic growth. And across the country there are demands led by national and local business pressure groups for roads investment significantly beyond the current programme.

Energy

There has been a massive shift in policy since the establishment of the Parliament on renewable energy thinking.

The Scottish Executive is currently consulting on setting a target that 40% of Scotland's electricity comes from renewables by 2020. The 40% target is a dramatic shift from the current '18% by 2010' target. It is worth remembering however, that the 18% target was itself seen as a radical first step in the early days of the Scottish Parliament. It was a step up from the 12% that the

Scottish Parliament inherited, which was largely met through post war hydro power.

As a result of the successful implementation of several wind energy projects, steady progress is being made to deliver on the current 18% target. The targets are important for their political significance – but they are also vital in sending out a clear message to the renewables industry that they can be confident that there is political support for sustained long-term renewables development in Scotland. The Vestas factory in Campbelton would not have been built without that clear signal from the Executive.

Writing at the launch of their 20:20 vision on the Future of Renewables in Scotland, the Scottish Renewables Forum identified the clear challenges of meeting the 40% target:

> There will be a need to bring on newer technologies; we will need to manage the grid much more actively, and we will need to ensure that the bulk of the jobs that deliver on these targets are created in Scotland. We also need to give serious consideration of the role of renewables in meeting our future transport and heating needs.

What we need is a 'route map' of how to achieve these wider goals, and what types of mechanisms and support will be needed to get there.

To date most of the political attention has rightly focused on wind because of the massive potential in Scotland. However, it is vital that we develop a balanced energy policy that acknowledges the different opportunities offered by a range of renewables technology. Wave technology still remains largely untapped and with our coastline we have excellent opportunities to develop sea and estuary based technology. As with wind there is a huge overseas market for the companies that develop the technology.

Discussions between the Scottish Executive and the UK Government about energy markets and investment in the grid are required. Action is also needed to deliver pricing mechanisms to enable very small scale renewables to export into the grid.

The announcement in January 2003 of the new Scottish Renewables Community Initiatives Fund represents a major opportunity for investment in solar heating, combined heat and power schemes, photovoltaics and biomass projects. The next step should be for more explicit targets and a change to building regulations and planning guidance to require not just higher energy efficiency performance but to encourage solar heating and embedded renewables.

Housing

One area where significant progress has been made on energy efficiency is via the March 2002 amendment to our building regulations. This has resulted in a 25-30% increase in energy standards bringing us more into line with northern European countries that share our climate.

The connections between fuel poverty and energy efficiency are also firmly on the agenda with progress now well underway on the Executive's programme on central heating for pensioners. The Warm Deal has meant that 120,000 low-income households have now got affordable heating and 400 New Deal places, as well as new jobs in the installation industry, have been created.

To date, there has only been experimental work using solar panels in Scotland as a long term source of fuel for households. However the new Scottish Communities Renewable Fund will deliver grant support for solar heating installations which could make them a viable financial proposition. In Parliamentary answers Margaret Curran, Social Justice Minister has indicated that this could be looked at in the housing stock transfer programme. There is also action now taking place to ensure that energy efficiency is considered in the major investment going into the building of new or replacement schools.

Waste

Local authorities in Scotland are now implementing the National Waste Strategy. But we are still at the bottom of the league table in Europe, recycling only 6% of our domestic waste. That means changing our wasteful throwaway culture, reducing the amount of waste we produce and making the maximum use of it through recycling and composting. However EU directives are positively forcing the pace for change.

It is significant that the first Area Waste Plans have come up with major emphasis on recycling and composting. That's where the maximum job creation is to be found with opportunities for local companies. While incineration is likely to be part of the solution it is vital that it is not seen as the cheap or easy replacement for landfill. That's why we need to promote recycling and learn from studies that show that people are prepared to act sensibly if we make it easy for them. That means we need more local opportunities for people to access recycling points.

In the debate on the Local Government Bill in Parliament we committed ourselves to include a target in the Bill to increase our recycling by 25% by 2006. This is an extremely challenging target – especially given that we are moving from a very low base point. But there are increasing numbers of local initiatives to test out how we make the difference.

I represent an inner city constituency with a much higher than average percentage of tenements. But there are now pilot projects being carried out to find the most effective model from the perspective of both householders and waste operators to deliver cost effective and efficient services that people will be able to use.

There is also interest in a project that would translate the lessons of waste management in Copenhagen in Denmark where there is a more holistic approach to managing tenement spaces by involving residents in maintaining spaces for community use, recycling, children's play areas and building in community safety.

'A lot done – a lot still to do'?

There has been some significant progress on issues such as housing, renewable energy, planning and transport, but more limited progress on waste, agriculture and economic development. On areas such as waste we are beginning to go in the right direction – but delivering on the ground is much harder.

Yet on agriculture and economic development there is still a very long way to go before environmental objectives find their way into mainstream policy development. Demands for a longer term commitment to organics and for a rewriting of agriculture strategy remain. On economic development, there is still a long way to go to persuade the business community as a whole of the merits of investing in environmental processes or thinking. After all we cannot make the cosy assumption that 'sustainable economy' automatically means '*environmentally* sustainable'.

Grounds for optimism

There have been important achievements – but is there room for optimism? The First Minister, Jack McConnell, was Labour's Environment Spokesperson in the run up to the 1999 Scottish Parliament elections and made a keynote speech on the Environment in February 2002, shortly after his election as First Minister.

His speech made the links between social and environmental justice – not remarkable in itself, as many of us have been making the connection for a long time. But his attendance at the Johannesburg Conference on Sustainable Development in the summer of 2002 underscored the seriousness with which the environment is now being taken by Labour in the Scottish Parliament.

The story is more complex when it comes to the question of sustainable development.

There is progress but we have a great deal still to do. One of my first acts as Transport and Environment Minister in 1999 was to set up a Ministerial Group on Sustainable Development. The aim was to focus on the extent to which Government Departments across the Executive were beginning to recognise sustainable development as central and to integrate thinking on the environment into the work that they did.

The Group has now evolved into a Cabinet Sub-Committee status giving it more status. However, there remains a major challenge in mainstreaming sustainable development across the Executive. 'Meeting the Needs: Priorities, Actions and Targets for Sustainable Development in Scotland' published in 2002 set 24 headline indicators, with the promise of more work to establish targets and the establishment of a Forum on Sustainable Development.

One key issue is rethinking our economic strategy for Scotland. We should highlight the potential for new jobs that can come from promotion of sectors such as organic foods, public transport, and renewable energy. But we've also got to make a difference with our core industries – electronics, manufacturing, service sector and tourism. Scottish business could benefit greatly from the wiser use of resources.

The Dow Jones Sustainable Group Index shows that firms that have adopted a more sustainable approach perform better than firms do generally. That should not come as a surprise. Firms that modernise their operations – are more efficient, save money on water and energy bills – become more competitive.

Environmental concerns must also be central to our agriculture strategy. EU policies underpin all UK agriculture, and EU policy is in favour of future agriculture support shifting to less intensive and more environmentally friendly forms of agriculture.

The Executive's organic action plan for Scotland should let us match the ambition shown by the UK Labour Government and countries across the EU where aspirational targets are in place, backed by marketing, training and changes to agricultural support.

We are still some way from having environment or sustainable development debates seen as important by the media or indeed across more than a relatively select group of MSPs and NGOs.

I accept that it can be difficult to get a handle on some of the important issues. Biodiversity is never going to feel as real or important to colleagues as creating jobs or eliminating poverty. But the connections have to be made.

The language of environmental justice begins to make the point that our bad old habits of environmental degradation, of over-reliance on landfill, incineration of waste, unfettered open cast mining, cold, damp housing and the resultant poor health are the reality for many of our constituents in Labour's traditional heartlands. Communities are being denied a decent environment.

So there are challenges in meeting the policy and process changes that are required to make the long term changes that cannot be brought about by the flick of a switch.

I firmly believe that we need a Cabinet-level Minister dedicated to the Environment – with Deputy Ministerial back up. There should be departmental targets on Sustainable Development regularly reported to a Ministerial Cabinet Sub-committee. An external Scottish Sustainable Development Forum should help set the agenda and act as a sounding board.

One of the successes of the Parliament has been the input of civic groups and environmental and business organisations to the development of policy and legislation, particularly through the committees of the Parliament. The recent addition of sustainable flood management to the Water Services and Environment Bill provided the best example yet of how effective the environmental NGOs can be. A degree of trust, built up from previous discussions and debates enabled a commitment from Ministers, backbenchers and civil servants which meant we got both the aspiration and the detail right.

The Scottish Parliament's Equal Opportunities Committee offers a model of how the consideration of sustainable development implications can be integrated more as part of the process of legislative, financial and policy scrutiny. While the first term of the Parliament has seen a great deal of emphasis, quite rightly, on modernising Scotland's legal framework, there should be a focus in the second term on review and monitoring of the impact of the implementation of these new laws.

A second term should see the detailed work required to deliver on our renewable energy aspirations. The shift from 18% to 40% on renewables will be a real challenge.

We should see further legislation to modernise our planning and nature conservation systems.

Current EU Directives will require the implementation of Strategic Environmental Assessment by July 2004. This will reinforce the need to embed environmental criteria in decision making. The 2002 Spending Review began the process of making explicit the impact and contribution of Scottish Executive spending. That process must be monitored and made more transparent.

We should aspire not just to wait until we are required to respond to environmental initiatives from the European Union, but make a virtue of innovation and high standards.

Then we will be able to feel a sense of pride not just in our hills and mountains – but also in our towns and cities too.

3

The green movement, Green Party
and economic change in Scotland

MARK BALLARD

Box 1

We in Scotland must accept our share of the responsibility for stabilising,
and then gradually reducing, resource consumption and waste production
to sustainable levels. We also recognise our responsibility to future
generations to conserve the Earth's resources so that they too may share
fully in its riches.

We wish to promote local community enterprise and personal
initiative, where enterprises are owned and controlled by those who work
in them and where they meet local needs. We recognise that inward
investment, particularly from multinational corporations, is not always in
the best interests of our economy. We envisage Scotland gradually gaining
greater control over her own resources, with a more diverse, flexible and
stable economy organised around people and their needs.

The Scottish Green Party wants an independent Scottish Parliament to
thoroughly reform our tax and benefits system, in order to promote a
green society based on social equity and ecological sustainability. Key
elements to this would be the introduction of the Citizens' Income Scheme
(CIS) and a Land Value Tax (LVT).

Green Economics in Scotland: a summary taken
from the SGP manifesto 2001

A personal and political context

This article is written not only as contribution to the debate on
what an agenda for a sustainable economy for Scotland would
look like, but also as a contribution to the debate on economics
within the green movement. Although I am a member of the
Council of the Scottish Green Party I do not speak on the party's

behalf (otherwise this article would merely be a copy of the manifesto, see Box 1).

Since the election of Robin Harper to the Scottish Parliament the Scottish Green Party's policies have come under much greater public scrutiny. This article therefore seeks to show how links can be made between our aspirations as a part of the wider green movement and the realities faced by a political party.

About the author

To put this article in a personal as well as a political context, I'm going to give a brief background to how I became involved in politics, leading to my involvement with the Green Party. This is not because my path is in any way unique, in fact I think it is of interest because it is so typical of many greens.

Like many in the Green Party I have a background on the left. In my case my first involvement in politics came when I was recruited by the Trotskyite Militant Tendency aged 15. Like most recruits I only stayed for a couple of years before drifting away. Looking back, the reasons why we drifted away were threefold. Firstly, the sterility of the political activities run by the Militant – endless paper sales and 'perspectives' meetings – which we came to feel were dull, repetitive and ineffectual. This was linked to the second problem: Militant had no clear vision of the post-revolutionary socialist society, or of how our work was contributing to it. Thirdly, like other Marxist organisations Militant dogmatically insisted that the class struggle was the only real struggle, and a classless society would be free of all oppression. This did not ring true. Other forms of oppression – on the basis of gender, race and sexuality as well as 'oppression' of the non-human world through the exploitation of nature seemed to us to have very real existence outside and parallel to the class struggle rather than being merely adjuncts to it.

However I stayed a member of the Labour party, as the main vehicle of opposition to Thatcher, and when I got to university worked to get a Labour government elected in 1992. Kinnock's defeat was a crushing blow, especially as it became clear that the Labour party's response would be to head even further right. So I left the Labour Party, which was a great wrench.

I still considered myself a socialist (I still do), and therefore wanted to continue to work for political change, but the other revolutionary left groups seemed to offer variations on Militant. However, the green movement, which was growing dramatically at that time, offered a politics that appeared more exciting, with interesting ideas about a future society and an openness to other ideas. A key element was Direct Action – the idea that you could change things by your own efforts, rather than waiting to capture state power, From permaculture gardening to occupying offices and GM crop pulls I found the experience of self-empowerment through direct action profoundly liberating.

So in contrast to the Trotskyites, the green movement offered a politics that attempted to link the green society of the future with green action in the present. It recognised that as well as a new economic relationship (the end of class oppression) other new relationships – with ourselves, with communities and nature – would have to be built.

After I left university I worked for a variety of radical non-government organisations, most recently as editor of the *Reforesting Scotland* Journal. *Reforesting Scotland* started life as an environmental organisation, promoting the virtues of tree-planting. However its brief has widened to encompass the wider environmental, economic and social benefits of ecological restoration. Restoring the trees, they argue must go hand in hand with restoring the people. Local people would manage the natural resources for the long-term benefit of all, diversify and developing the economy and environment. It is a powerful vision of community action through empowering communities.

The Green Party

After the euphoria of the Scottish Parliament referendum victory in 1997, like many in the green movement in Scotland, I realised that the subsequent PR elections could be an important venue for promoting green ideas. In this context I should mention that an important part of the vision of the Green Party was that it saw itself as a political voice for the movement. Unlike the traditional radical left parties it doesn't see itself as the movement or even as the sole political voice of the movement. Within this wider green movement there are some tools that political parties can do that other groups can't – i.e. stand candidates for election. I am a firm believer in the 'use every tool in the box' approach – non-government organisations, single-issue campaigns, direct action groups and political parties can all do different things – but I believe we are all part of the movement towards the same goals. Of course this means that the party has to recognise where its limits are – there is no point in the Green Party replicating work better done by single issue campaigns.

However being in a political party also gives you a focus on issues of how power is distributed in society. This is sometimes something important that we can bring to the wider green movement. Equally the way the Green Party operates is itself informed by the way the rest of the movement has developed, with a strong ethos of consensus, grassroots democracy and putting ideas directly into action.

Towards a green economy

Where do discussions of green economics start? The first principle is that all human economic activity and social and cultural wellbeing depend on the maintenance of our natural environment. Greens argue that our continually increasing extraction of resources from our environment, together with the growing pollution of this environment is ever-more incompatible with ecological sustainability.

However, not only does our current economic system fail Scotland's environment, it also fails the people of Scotland. One third of the children in Scotland grow up in poverty. Scotland's diet is amongst the worst in Europe – largely a reflection of the limited choice those in poverty have over where they can shop, what they can pay and what is available. Social justice and environmental sustainability are intimately linked. While there are gross inequalities in the distribution of wealth and power in society, the achievement of a truly sustainable society is impossible.

Greens argue that economic power must therefore be devolved to the lowest appropriate level. By putting people in charge of their own economic destiny people will no longer be vulnerable to the damaging effects of economic decisions made elsewhere and over which they have no control. This would liberate and empower all sections of society to meet their needs as far as possible from their own resources through activities which are socially enhancing. The key must be to allow all to contribute to society according to their abilities, recognising as they do so, responsibility for themselves, for others, for future generations and for the planet.

A sustainable economic policy for Scotland must therefore promote the emergence of an economic system which recognises the limits of, and is compatible with, both the natural systems of the planet and the aspirations of the all its people.

Beyond the 'market mechanism' versus 'state control'

Greens argue that a central problem with our current economic system is that it is system rather than needs driven. Companies exist to sell more of their products, no matter what human needs are fulfilled by these products. Markets are efficient ways of distributing goods and services, but pay no attention to the social or environmental impacts of these goods and services. This is a familiar critique from socialists as well as greens. However, greens argue that many socialist proposals for a new system of distribution, in which the state is central, end up creating a new system that is equally system driven. State planning systems across the world have shown themselves to be unresponsive to needs, often generating bureaucracies whose main concern is self–preservation rather than meeting any societal need.

In keeping with our belief in local democracy and decentralisation, greens see the solution lying in local economies, based on community-controlled economic enterprises. Rather than a simple axis of left versus right, greens therefore see a third axis of centralisation and decentralisation, and place community rather than state or market at the heart of their thinking (fig 3.1).

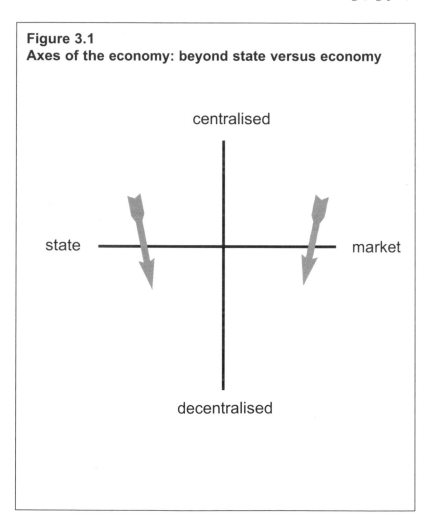

Figure 3.1
Axes of the economy: beyond state versus economy

Saving the environment without destroying quality of life

As a Green Party member, the depressingly common reaction I get when I talk about green economics is 'you want us all to go back to hunting and gathering, don't you'. One of the main reasons why so many in Scotland are in denial about the unsustainable nature of our economy is based on the mistaken assumption that a sustainable economy means a reduction in their quality of life. We must not forget that we have to demonstrate that a sustainable economy will have a higher quality of life – that it is possible to consume less while increasing real wealth. We must demonstrate that green alternatives will lead to a less stressful, healthier and more enjoyable life.

How much is health worth? A recent study conducted by University of Warwick looked at what life events such as marriage, divorce and widowhood were worth in financial terms. The study found that marriage brings the same amount of happiness as a £70,000 a year income, but a major decline in health is equivalent to a loss of £500,000 a year. People in Scotland suffer from very high levels of stress-related illness – in 2001 depression was the most common condition recorded by Scottish family doctors at 152 cases per 1,000 members of the population. Hypertension came in second with 143 cases per 1,000 of the population. So therefore greens argue, since a less competitive and consumerist economy will be less stressful, a green economy will improve health and hence quality of life.

The stage beyond this is to re-orientate science and technological research to look at more resource efficient models of production. Commercial pressures have driven research towards technologies that are very resource intensive, since financial profitability rather than resource sustainability have been the main goals. It has been argued that using existing or near-existing technology it would be possible to half Scotland's resource use while simultaneously doubling wealth. This would however require a major shift in research priorities – which could only come if it was part of a wider shift away from prioritising profit.

Realo or fundi?

The green movement in Scotland and the world has become very effective in highlighting the problems caused by the current economic system and its increasing destruction of communities and the environment. However, it has often struggled to articulate what its alternative economy would look like. Indeed the most common criticism of the 'anti-globalisation/anti-capitalist' movement of recent years has been its failure (or refusal) to propose clear alternative models. Greens have tended to mistrust over-arching economic models (often after negative experiences of Marxism), instead emphasising a diversity of forms and structures.

The danger is that, without a clear vision of a future economy, the green movement falls into the trap of pure reformism – tinkering with the existing system to counteract some of its worst excesses, without changing the underlying logic of the system. This has been referred to as 'changing the light bulbs on the Titanic'. The German Green Party has found that involvement first in parliament, and then in government has caused great tension between its radical aspirations and limited achievements, between the 'fundi' and 'realo' tendencies. It has been argued that this was partly because the German Greens did not have a clear enough programme to take into coalition negotiations, and so were easily sidetracked into minor reforms.

However the scale of the changes needed to make our economy sustainable are sometimes overwhelming. For example Scotland, with an economy based on fossil fuels, will probably have to reduce its carbon dioxide emissions by sixty to eighty percent to achieve a sustainable level of use. Demands of this scale are hard to reconcile with the current political discourse, which baulks at even achieving the Kyoto target of stabilisation of carbon dioxide emissions. This has led some in the green movement to retreat from attempts to change the existing economy and simply argue that the system must be overturned in its entirety. However, this can lead to a politics that has little contact with the day-to-day realities of everyday life.

The task for the green movement is to develop an alternative economic strategy for Scotland (and equally importantly a way of promoting that alternative) which is both connected to the realities of existing politics, while recognizing the wholesale nature of the required change in the system.

Box 2

Birse Community Trust (BCT) is a new community business that has been set up 'to promote the common good of the inhabitants of Birse parish and deliver wider benefits'. Birse parish covers over 12,500 hectares of Deeside and has four main parts: the three scattered rural communities of Finzean, Ballogie and Birse and the largely uninhabited Forest of Birse, which covers a quarter of the parish's entire area. BCT is a Company Limited by Guarantee and a recognised Scottish charity. Everyone on the Electoral Registers for Birse is automatically a voting member of BCT and thus responsible, among other matters, for electing BCT's Board of Trustees.

BCT is a local response to the changing nature of the support available to rural communities. Traditionally, in parishes like Birse, nearly everyone was a tenant of a large private estate, and for most community needs the communities turned to the estate for support. In the post-war period, as estates became less able (or willing) to perform this role, communities looked increasingly to the Local Authorities for support. Recently, as Local Authorities have become more constrained rural communities have had to develop their own initiatives. Thus the first reason for establishing BCT was as a vehicle for community projects and to access funding.

The second reason was the need to have a local common good trust as part of resolving long-standing local issues about who had what rights over the area known as the Forest of Birse Commonty.

Robin Callander, *Reforesting Scotland Journal* issue 24

Building the new economy

Birse Community Trust (Box 2) is a good example of the new generation of localised community economic enterprises. It recognises that neither private sector approaches, in this case relying on the munificence of the local laird, nor state sector, in this case the local authority, will meet the needs of the local community. BCT is a company, but has charitable objectives. It is rooted in the community – membership is conferred by virtue of residence within the community. It is also a mechanism for overcoming old issues over ownership and rights to use natural resources.

As outlined in the previous section, relying on neither 'the big state' nor 'the big market' will be the key to the sustainable transformation of Scotland's economy. Instead, I argued, we must develop localised community economic enterprises, that bring economic decision making down to the most appropriate level and promote self reliance within communities and regions. These localised initiatives offer the best way to enable more local needs to be met by local work using local resources. As David Korten puts it in *When Corporations ruled the world,* 'Communism vested property rights in a distant state and denied people any means of holding the state accountable for the exercise of these rights, while capitalism persistently transfers property rights to giant corporations and financial institutions that are largely unaccountable even to their owners'.

There are a wide range of alternative local economic initiatives that have a part to play in the new economy. However my task in this article is not to promote any particular scheme, but instead to look from a policy perspective at what can be done to aid all these alternative, localised, community, economic initiatives.

As a first step we will look at what the government is doing in this area.

Current government policy and the social economy

The government strategy of promoting inward investment by high-tech firms in Scotland, seen as the solution to the decline in traditional heavy industry, is now falling apart. Major companies like NEC, Motorola, IBM and Hyundai which were attracted to Scotland by this policy over the last three decades have all now shut or significantly downscaled their Scottish operations.

The result has been a growing government interest in the social economy and social entrepreneurs. These economic initiatives are being touted as a solution to a wide range of problems. Even Tony Blair has thrown his weight behind it – in a recent (English) Department of Trade and Industry report *Social Enterprise – a strategy for success* he declared 'By combining strong public service ethos with business acumen, we can open up the possibility of entrepreneurial organizations – highly responsive to customers and with the freedom of the private sector – but which are driven by a commitment to public benefit rather than purely maximising profits for shareholders'. The Government believes there is significant potential for more public services to be delivered by social enterprises, and that local authorities in particular have an important role in opening up procurement processes.

So what does the government mean by the social economy? It could be defined as being made up of non-state economic enterprises which have objectives other than profit and return on capital. Typically these objectives are to benefit the community or wider society. Examples of social economy organisations include Community Trusts like Birse Community Trust mentioned above, smaller co-operatives and industrial provident societies, charitable companies and 'social firms'. (The term 'social firm' is used to describe a business created for the employment of people with a disability or other disadvantage in the labour market).

This social economy agenda is quite different from Corporate Social Responsibility, which aims to encourage companies to act in a way that combines profitability with respect for ethical values, people, communities and the environment. Unlike the social economy, production is still 'for profit', and ultimately profit must take precedence over social responsibility. However the two ideas are linked – by developing the idea that business can have responsibilities other than profit maximisation and return on shareholder capital.

Going beyond the government's approach

It is very positive that the current government has begun to recognise the potential for the social economy. This represents a major opportunity for the green movement. We must develop strategies for moving towards a sustainable economy which recognises the scale of the changes required while remaining connected to existing politics. The government interest in this area is a potential for such a bridge between existing policy and our radical vision.

However, the government appears to see the social economy in quite limited terms. The role of the Green Party should therefore be to expose the limits of the government's vision and challenge them politically. This must be linked to the direct action that individuals and communities are taking to develop alternative economic initiatives on the ground. Strong networks of these groups are need to promote the potential of the new economy, and to build support structure. The Green Party can then campaign in ways that even the strongest networks of these groups couldn't – by directly challenging government economic policy and proposing alternatives.

A green critique

One of the problems for the government in dealing with social enterprise is that it doesn't fit neatly into any of the traditional social/voluntary, state and the enterprise/economic sectors. Government thinking tends to focus on ways that social enterprise can replace existing voluntary sector provision – adding entrepreneurial flair to charities, and replacing state sector provision.

A good example of what the government has in mind is the Glasgow Housing Association (GHA) which took over from Glasgow Council as the landlord of council houses in Glasgow following the ballot of council tenants in 2002. GHA is an Industrial & Provident Society registered with the Registrar of Friendly Societies. It is a not-for-profit organization, with any surplus generated reinvested. Half the members of the Voluntary Management Committee are elected tenants (the other half are four Glasgow Councilors, an MSP and an MP and three independents). A central aim of GHA 'is to promote local community empowerment, control and ownership.

'Choices will be available to tenants in exercising greater devolved management and opportunities for community ownership. In terms of devolved management, tenants will move to a local management arrangement provided by a new Local Housing Organisation or an existing community-based Housing Association according to their choice.'

How does the government-promoted GHA model compare to Birse Community Trust, which I mentioned at the start as an example of the green vision of community economic initiatives? There are three glaring differences. The first is in scale. GHA will be a huge organisation covering the whole of Glasgow – BCT relates to a community. An organisation the size of GHA will find it very difficult to respond to local needs, and avoid becoming overly bureaucratic and system-driven. Secondly BCT is entirely owned by its members, while only half of GHA's members are tenants. Even then assuring that these tenant's representatives are actually accountable will be very difficult to maintain when dealing with such a large organisation. Finally the stock renewal process will involve borrowing at least £770 million from the banks, effectively making the project part of the Private Finance Initiative. The GHA will therefore be in hock to the banks, who as the creditors may well come effectively to determine the project's direction in line with what ensures the return of their loans.

So greens would argue that for the social economy to deliver its promise it must be based around community structures and owned and managed by the community. The challenge this represents should not be underestimated. People are unused to the responsibility of self management. Although communities exist across Scotland, it takes a lot of work in places like Birse to strengthen community feeling to the level where it becomes possible to talk about 'the community'. Again the Scottish Green Party seeks to work hand in hand with communities to develop capacity within communities. The experience of community organisations across the world has demonstrated the amazing potential to be found within communities when people are supported and trusted in taking over responsibility for their lives.

What needs to happen

In *Social Enterprise – a strategy for success*, mentioned above, the government laid out a set of key policies as part of a strategy for successful development of social enterprise. These included:

- Research size, strength and spread of social enterprise
- Remove regulatory, tax and administrative barriers
- Improve access to training, finance and funding
- Raising awareness and celebrating success of social enterprise
- Develop and agree minimum standards of behaviour or an accreditation system

The Scottish Green Party would urge the Scottish Executive to adopt these polices, and support and encourage action to implement the above measures. Taken together with a recognition of the issues of size and control mentioned above they would represent a significant step forward in promoting sustainable economic agenda for Scotland.

However greens argue that the third issue raised by the example of GHA and BCT has not been fully taken into account, that of changing the wider economic context. Certainly social enterprises may have a role in taking on a function currently administered by the state or by voluntary groups, if the issues of size and ownership are taken into account. Social enterprises have however perhaps their greatest potential in taking over areas that are currently part of the 'enterprise' sector – directly challenging traditional for-profit businesses. Only if social enterprises are supported in expanding into this sector can the social economy come to assume the role that even Tony Blair ascribed to it, of transforming the economy to make enterprise 'driven by a commitment to public benefit rather than purely maximising profits for shareholders'.

To achieve this expansion of social enterprise a major shift will be required in the attitude and orientation of Scottish Enterprise and Highlands and Islands Enterprise. There is limited staff understanding and awareness of the needs of not-for-profit business. This lack of awareness is probably matched in existing voluntary sector support structures, which have the opposite problem – a lack of awareness and understanding of the needs of business, even not–for-profit business. Across government economic and social policy therefore there needs to be a commitment to supporting the establishment of social enterprises. This must go together with a major shift of power and responsibility from government to these community owned and controlled enterprises. Such moves to support certain kinds of business because of their internal structure (not-for profit and community ownership and management) could fall foul of commitments the British government has entered into with the European Union and World Trade Organisation, which are based on principles of free trade rather than supporting local initiatives. However Scotland would not be alone promoting these kinds social enterprises. Many other countries are seeing a rapid growth in local, community and not-for-profit economic initiatives in response to the destructive influence of globalisation.

Problems with the socialised economy

Can social enterprise be as efficient as traditional business? An economy based purely on profit maximising will find it difficult to take account of social or environmental needs, which by their very nature cannot be easily quantified in financial terms. However the profit mechanism does act as an effective external discipline. If your profit is not growing as fast or faster than your competition you will either be taken over or go under. In theory this pressure from the market should stop management becoming complacent, concentrating on self preservation and internal systems rather than meeting the needs of customers. Without the pressure to maximise profits, what will ensure that social enterprises do not become complacent and unresponsive?

As I outlined above one of the key green criticisms of both traditional left and right politics is on the basis of scale. Greens argue that the fact that social enterprises will be small scale, rooted in local communities, will act as a discipline. Community enterprises can be directly responsible to the people they effect, and therefore more responsive to a range of social and environmental as well as economic needs.

Can a social enterprise run a railway?

This discipline may work for small companies, but what about enterprises that have to be larger than a community? In 1999 out of 299,200 enterprises operating in Scotland, 293,765 (98 per cent) had fewer than 50 employees. These enterprises, together with medium sized enterprise (50-249 employees) accounted for 67 per cent of total Scottish private employment. At the same time, whilst there were only 2,170 large enterprises – with 250 employees or more – operating in Scotland (0.7 per cent of the total), these represented 43 per cent of total Scottish private employment. Approximately 192,000 of Scottish enterprises were sole traders or partnerships without employees, leaving around 107,000 larger enterprises.

A local ownership and management structure may be appropriate for the small and medium enterprises, but it is difficult to see how it could be applied to the small number of larger firms that operate on a Scotland-wide basis. The benefits of social and community ownership – that enterprises are locally based and therefore responsive to local conditions and needs – will not apply. Can a social enterprise run a railway?

This question does have a great deal contemporary political relevance. The UK Government is currently wrestling with the problem of trying to run a railway to fulfil a range of economic social and environmental benefits which clearly make it inappropriate to be run on a for-profit basis.

I think it is important that we remember why the greens support social enterprises in the first place. Social enterprises are laboratories of alternative economic experimentation. They help to develop new capacities in communities, and alternative economic structures, that can help to move us towards a more sustainable future. Trying to apply the social enterprise model to larger and larger structures will in the end fail as the model becomes increasingly less relevant. Trying to fit the social economy model to these large structures may also prove to be a distraction from the central task of developing local structures. In many ways it is simpler to set up a body like GHA than a large number of small community-owned and managed social enterprises. But it is the smaller social enterprises that have the most potential – setting up GHA will not prove to be an effective short cut.

Conclusion: how far can social enterprise go?

The proposals outlined above for identifying what it is about social enterprise that is important, and support these elements, will not in themselves lead to a sustainable Scotland. But if the key to a sustainable Scotland is to put people in charge of their own destinies, to bring the economy to a community level and to allow people to manage and interact with their environments in locally appropriate and sustainable ways then social enterprise may prove to be an important way of building the capacity to do this. Supporting social enterprise offers a flexible model, which individuals and communities can adapt to meet local needs. Its strength will come from the participants themselves, taking direct action to improve their lives. As such it is something that the Scottish Green Party must promote widely across Scotland.

The new safety net – reforming fiscal policy to protect people and the planet

Taxation is needed in order to fund public expenditure – financing the schools and hospitals we all need. Traditional politics, as a battle between left and right, has been cast as a battle between 'tax-cutting Tories' and 'Tax-and-spend' Labour. Since the Labour government of the 1970s there has been increasing economic consensus between the major political parties in Britain. At times the gap between the parties has been no wider than a penny on income tax. As a Green Party, in our quest for a socially just and environmentally sustainable society, we have to intervene in political discussions on overall taxation policy and point out ways in which tax structures can be altered to help bring about a sustainable society. The raising of funds is not the only purpose of taxation – the way they are raised is crucial in determining the wider social, environmental and economic impacts of those taxes.

There is a tendency for opposition parties to simply demand more taxation, or the introduction of certain specific forms of taxation to meet the cost of their particular spending priority. What I am proposing is that a key part of the agenda for a sustainable Scotland is a major overhaul of our fiscal structure – how we raise taxes and what we spend them on – rather than a series of ad-hoc measures.

Taxation is usually divided into direct and indirect forms. Direct taxation applies to the wealth of individuals, families or companies, whether as income, capital or inheritance. Indirect taxation applies to activities or goods or services, rather than directly to wealth. Direct taxation, in conjunction with benefits payments, can be used to create greater social equity and justice. Indirect taxation can be used to try to alter consumption patterns and create ecological sustainability. The purpose of a sustainable taxation policy should not be to shift the overall relative burden of taxation either towards direct or towards indirect taxation. Instead, the aim is to alter our approaches to both forms of taxation so that it is better suited to help bring about a green society.

In general, indirect taxation is regressive, i.e. it impacts relatively more heavily on the poorer members of society than those who are more wealthy. In this way, indirect taxation works against the creation of social equity and, therefore, against the aims of a green society. For this reason such taxes should not be levied unless their intention is to help bring about ecological sustainability or to address concerns about other social issues such as public health.

The main forms of direct taxation currently in use are Income Tax (including National Insurance), Inheritance and Capital Gains Tax, and Corporation Tax on business. The main indirect tax is Value Added Tax, although there are some moves towards resource taxes, such as the Climate Change Levy. Box 3 explains the Scottish Green Party approach to these taxes. However the distinctive contribution of green thinking to fiscal policy lies in the Citizens' Income Scheme and the shift to resource taxation at national and local levels.

Citizens' Income

The Citizens' Income Scheme is an effective way of simplifying the current tax and benefit system, while helping to move society to a more sustainable notion of work. Under this scheme every person would receive a basic income from the state. It would be set at a level high enough to allow people to provide their basic needs of shelter, food, clothing and heating from this source alone. This income is non-taxable, and would replace the personal tax

Box 3

Direct Taxation

Income Tax

Income Tax is the instrument by which all citizens who are able to are required to contribute a proportion of their labour to the running of public services. It is also, when combined with benefits payments, the primary way in which wealth can be redistributed in order to create a fairer society.

A sustainable economic policy for Scotland would simplify the tax system, while reducing the current tax breaks on unearned income. The current maze of income tax, national insurance, personal allowances, welfare benefits and tax credits would be abolished and replaced with a system of Citizens' Income (see below) and income tax levied on all income above the Citizens' Income. Tax rates will be banded and will increase progressively so that those on higher incomes are paying higher marginal rates of tax.

The distinction between 'earned' and 'unearned' income will no longer be used to determine different methods of direct taxation. For example National Insurance is a form of income tax in disguise, but as it is only levied on 'earnings' (i.e. wages and self-employment income), it means that 'unearned' investment income is currently taxed at a lower rate than 'earned' income. Under a green taxation system, National Insurance will be abolished as a separate entity and merged into general Income Tax.

Inheritance/ Capital Gains Tax

Both these taxes effectively ensure that unearned income is taxed at a lower rate than earned income. While there are certain areas where taxes on realisation of investments should be taxed at a lower rate or not at all, for example the sale of one's main home, in general income tax should be paid on all profits of the sale of investment assets. Equally capital losses will reduce a person's taxable income.

Inheritance Tax should be reformed so that it is calculated on a 'recipient basis' (i.e. with reference to the circumstances of the person receiving the inheritance rather than the donor). It should also be extended to include gifts made during a donor's lifetime, rather than just those given as inheritances on death, therefore becoming an accessions tax. There should be an annual exemption/threshold for amounts received as gifts or inheritances. Inheritance Tax rates should be progressively banded, with rates of tax increasing according to a recipient's total income/wealth. Recipients who only pay Income Tax at lower rates would not be subject to Inheritance Tax.

The tax-free threshold will be sufficient to ensure that most ordinary gifts between members of families with moderate incomes will not be taxed, and, as gifts will be averaged over a five year period, it will also allow for larger 'one-off' gifts (such as those received on marriage, or given by parents to their offspring to help them buy a house).

Private trusts will be taxed at a single uniform rate on all assets transferred into them and profits made by them. There will be no annual exemption/threshold for trusts. Distributions from trusts to beneficiaries will be taxed according to the recipient's circumstances, in accordance with the policies laid out above.

As with Capital Gains Tax, a person's only or main home will be exempt from Inheritance Tax. If a person inherits a property which is already their principal private residence there will be no Inheritance Tax to pay.

Corporation Tax

Corporation Tax will continue to be levied on the net profits earned by companies. These will be banded, with higher rates payable by larger companies in order to encourage smaller businesses.

Some businesses operating within the UK do not currently pay UK taxes because they are able to transfer their profits abroad to have them taxed there. The loopholes would be closed so that company profits earned in the UK were taxed here, even where this would mean that profits of trans-national corporations may be taxed twice – once in the UK and again in a foreign country.

Indirect Taxation

VAT

VAT is the largest revenue provider of all the current indirect taxes. It is often referred to as a tax on 'consumption', whereas it is more accurately described as a tax on the spending of money. In conventional economic terms these might be seen to be the same thing, but to greens the word 'consumption' implies the using up of the world's valuable resources and this is the type of consumption that we would wish to tax in order to encourage resource conservation.

The current system of VAT is regressive and is not intended to bring about any ecological benefits. It therefore does not fit with the principles of green taxation. It is also highly bureaucratic and a severe burden on many small businesses. For these reasons VAT should be phased out and replaced with a system of environmental taxation measures ('eco-taxes'). These will target specific products, production methods, resources used and pollutants produced in order to discourage ecologically unsustainable consumption.

allowance and most welfare benefits (other than those for special needs). Further income would then be taxed on a progressive scale. Students in further and higher education would receive the basic income, effectively restoring student maintenance grants.

Citizens' Income Scheme has a number of important benefits. It would end the current confusing and inefficient overlap of tax and benefit payments that are administered by the UK Treasury and the UK Department of Social Security respectively. These departments are separate and have different objectives. As a result, incentives to work are distorted. A low-paid worker wanting to work more to increase earnings may gain nothing, or perhaps even lose, if benefits are lost and tax becomes payable (the 'poverty trap'). An unemployed individual may be worse off by taking a job for similar reasons (the 'unemployment trap'). Since the basic income in the CIS is guaranteed, and partly financed by the abolition of most welfare benefits, these disincentives to work cannot occur. A decision to work in paid employment, or work more hours in paid employment, will increase income. This will apply to both full and part-time employment.

The CIS will also allow more people to provide socially useful work in 'unpaid' sectors of the economy. An unemployed or part-time employed person may find it difficult to undertake voluntary work under the current tax and benefits system because such work may reduce his or her entitlement to benefits.

The CIS will also recognise the value of activities such as caring for relatives by providing a basic income to those involved, rather than requiring them to claim benefits. It would encourage more flexible working patterns, allowing people to determine for themselves how much paid work they wish to do. Job-sharing and part-time working, which are often made impossible by the current tax and benefits system, would become more feasible options. The more flexible labour market that will develop under the CIS will also increase the economic independence of women with and without children by increasing women's opportunities for employment (see Duffin, this volume).

Eco-taxes

Environmental tax measures ('eco-taxes') are designed to encourage movement towards a sustainable economy, by increasing the prices of items or services produced using unsustainable or polluting practices. They will therefore be calculated to achieve the desired environmental effects, not to maximise revenue. It is acknowledged that environmental taxation can only be successful when integrated with a great many other measures, including regulation where necessary. Eco-taxes should be levied as close to the point of production as is practical. Resource taxation will be charged on the use of raw materials, and will reflect their relative scarcity and the environmental disruption caused by extraction.

It is very important to prevent taxes on fossil fuels from impacting too heavily on the poorest members of society through their domestic fuel bills. Therefore households should be given a tax-free (or cost-free) initial fuel allowance which will vary according to the season to reflect basic heating needs. Fuel suppliers will no longer be allowed to levy standing charges for fuel supply, nor to give price discounts for increased fuel use. In this way, the amount paid by the customer for increased fuel use will better reflect the environmental impact. Again this would have to go hand in hand with a great many other policy measures to tackle fuel poverty and improve energy efficiency of homes in Scotland.

As well as taxing the use of resources which are input into a production process, taxes should also be levied on the outputs of those processes, according to their ecological impact. This will include taxes levied on the desired products of manufacture if they are considered pollutants (e.g. pesticides or plastic packaging products) as well as taxes on waste products and emissions (e.g. toxic gases) which are discharged into the surrounding environment. In the case of fossil fuels, a tax based on the carbon content of the fuel (and therefore subsequent CO_2 emissions) would discourage their use and reduce their effect on climate change.

Import duties will be levied on both raw materials and finished products which will reflect the ecological impact of the production, extraction and transportation of such goods where sufficient eco-taxes are not considered to have been levied in their country of origin. This system will include a re-introduction of duties on goods imported from other European Union countries where considered necessary. Enforcement procedures exercised by Customs and Excise must be sufficient to prevent a rise in organised crime in relation to smuggling and evasion of duties.

Local Government Finance

Local Government Finance has been a controversial issue in Scotland for many years. An effective system of Local Government Finance should combine an element of social justice with a relationship to the local area (for example the Council tax/rates relating to property within the local authority area.

A Land Value Tax (LVT) combines these two elements very effectively. Ownership of land confers significant benefits, but in Scotland these benefits are very unfairly distributed. LVT is charged according to the value of these benefits, and is therefore a socially just and locally related tax. It would also help to create a more equitable the pattern of land holding in Scotland.

A tax on land values would be paid by all landholders to the local authority, and would replace Council Tax and the Uniform Business Rate, and would include rural land. It would be charged on the value of land, regardless of what development has taken place on it.

This tax would help deal with a major problem with our current system of land use and ownership. At present the benefits of higher land values accrue only to the landowner. Increases in land value through factors such as the granting by the community of planning permission to build, or the development of surrounding areas because of increased community activity, create unearned benefit in the form of windfall profits for the landowner. The possibility of windfall profits also encourages speculators to buy land and hold it, often unused or under-used, with little benefit to the community. LVT would capture these windfall profits and redistribute them to the local community. LVT would thus discourage land ownership for speculative purposes only, and promote a fuller use of land within the existing planning constraints.

A policy of taxing land values will give net benefits to many people, whether urban or rural, including owner-occupiers on small or medium plots, and those who do not own land. Reducing land speculation will make more land available at lower prices, encouraging the growth of smaller-scale community enterprises.

The amount of LVT paid depends on the activities that are feasible and permitted on the land in question, and for this reason LVT needs to be co-ordinated closely with the planning system. As well as being simple and cheap to administer, depending only on land value and planning controls, LVT is difficult to evade, since land cannot be physically transferred to low or zero tax countries.

Conclusions

Now that the green movement has achieved parliamentary representation in Scotland it provides many opportunities, but also risks. The diversity of the movement is great and, as Germany has shown, divisions can occur when faced with the realities of political responsibility. However, the diversity of the movement is also its strength, putting into practice something of the radical democracy of the direct action practitioners, whilst at the same time taking responsibility for running an ecologically and socially just economy.

I have argued that a sustainable economic policy for Scotland must promote the emergence of an economic system which recognises the limits of, and is compatible with, both the natural systems of the planet and the aspirations of the all its people. This economy must be based on community-controlled economic enterprises that seek to empower local people. It must base it's appeal on the very real improvements to quality of life that can be realised through a less consumerist and competitive economy. A strategy for achieving this policy must recognise the wholesale nature of the required change in the system while remaining connected to the realities of existing politics.

4

Recognising Citizenship:
a new architecture for welfare

STUART DUFFIN

Principles of welfare

When the first Scottish Executive set up a Department of Social Justice, it arguably adopted a stronger position on social cohesion than Westminster. However, the principal policy tools for delivering social justice – taxation and state welfare – remain reserved powers. Reforms in the taxation and benefits systems have been carried out under New Labour to reflect changing demographic and ideological conditions. Here it is argued that aspects of these have been valuable, but remain inadequate, and that further reforms could significantly contribute to social cohesion through the introduction of a basic income.

Social cohesion is important in UK public policy for three sets of reasons. First, democratic politics can only flourish in a society which is in some sense a community (Hobhouse, 1922) – where citizens have something important in common that overrides their differences. In their various ways Northern Ireland, the former Yugoslavia and the Caucasus all illustrate this. Second, fundamental inequalities (of resources and of opportunities) generate wasteful conflicts and social problems, such as crime and other resistance activities by poor people, and even affect a society's average health and longevity. But third, the redistributive politics that make greater equality and social harmony possible in turn depend on a culture of sympathy, co-operation and mutual identification that has to be created, and certainly can't any longer be taken for granted. I want to focus on welfare state services (health, education, social care and income maintenance) as factors in the building of social cohesion, and hence in establishing the conditions for democratic politics.

In the post-war 'Golden Age' of welfare states, it was generally agreed in the UK and Europe, if not in the USA, that collective state provision for health and welfare was an important condition for stable democracy. In the UK, the Beveridge Report and the 1945 Labour government both appealed directly to our wartime shared experience of suffering and threat, to national unity in adversity. For the UK the war was an experience of successful pulling together that allowed collective institutions to be established in a highly individualistic political culture, where citizenship was (and is) about competence in holding one's own in competition with others. In Europe the reasons were slightly different. Democracy had not survived the class conflicts of the inter-war period. Both fascism and communism were totalitarian systems in which the state created social cohesion by suppressing opposition forces. Welfare states were therefore constructed as bulwarks for a democratic resolution of class antagonisms, as much through the co-operation of employers and workers over full-employment policies as for their redistributive effects (Rimlinger, 1973). So, continental democracy and collective institutions are about harmonising class interests more than establishing viable forms of individual equality between individual citizens.

Central to any welfare state is the relationship between taxation and welfare receipt. I would argue that there are eight principles that should guide any tax/welfare system. The first principle is that *nature and its resources are for the benefit of all*, that no-one should be excluded from participating in, and benefiting from, economic growth.

The second principle identified is *adequacy*. All citizens have a right to an income sufficient to live life with basic dignity. For this I describe poverty as, 'People are living in poverty if their income and resources (material, cultural and social) are so inadequate as to preclude them from having a standard of living which is regarded as acceptable by society generally. As a result of inadequate income and resources people may be excluded and marginalised from participating in activities which are considered the norm for other people in society.'

The third principle identified is that of *guarantee*. Knowing the level at which an adequate income should be set is not enough. This income level should be guaranteed. The only way this can be done is to place the guarantee on a statutory basis. Only then can we be sure that every citizen will receive an adequate income. It is important to note that having such a guarantee does not mean that all the income would have to come from the State. It could, for example, in whole or in part, come from payment for a job. The statutory guarantee would ensure that unemployed people and those in low-paid employment would be assured of a minimum income, which was adequate to live with dignity.

The fourth principle identified is that the adequate income must be provided on a *non-withdrawable* basis. Some welfare systems are experienced as degrading by many recipients. Some tax and welfare systems are linked in such a way that poverty traps are created and many unemployed people face income losses if they take up a job. An adequate income guarantee system should ensure that all receive the adequate income without encountering these or other penalties.

The fifth principle concerns *equity and equality*. This means that the system should promote both equity of treatment and outcome, including gender equality. This, in practice, would mean that inequalities in income would be reduced and resources transferred to ensure that everyone received the basic payment to which they were entitled. It would also involve an equitable sharing of the costs of such a system. Within this principle it would also follow that identical needs and circumstances should be dealt with identically.

The sixth principle identified concerns *efficiency*. Efficiency is not solely referring to economic efficiency; nor, that an adequate income guarantee system has to provide conditions that produce optimal growth. Rather, this system should have a positive impact, relative to the status quo, on both the situation of the worst-off in society and on the socio-economic situation as a whole.

The seventh principle concerns *simplicity*. As far as possible an adequate income system should be simple to understand and to administer. Many social welfare systems are complex. This complexity leads to an increase in administrative costs, constant confusion, delays and (unintended) victimisation. In practice, many people fail to claim their full entitlements.

The eighth principle proposed concerns *freedom*. An adequate income guarantee system should promote autonomy and reduce dependency. The present system forces many people into dependency. For example, some social welfare systems force people to do nothing as a condition of receiving their payment. This conditionality creates a dependency culture. In the case of couples receiving social welfare payments one is treated as a 'dependent' of the other. In most welfare systems people in receipt of payments lose benefits if they earn money through work, some even lose if they take up study. This reduces their autonomy. A more progressive system is required which encourages and promotes the involvement of every person in the social, economic, political and cultural life of the society.

Building a new architecture

As it stands the current system of tax/benefits is very complex. It gives every appearance of being designed by and for experts and it is certainly impossible for the majority of its users to understand. Moreover, it is not sufficiently flexible to create a secure platform for enabling people to enter the flexible labour market. Claimants are often unclear of the effect that taking work will have on their benefits – many assume that this will result in the loss of all benefit entitlements. Certainly many have no means of knowing how much benefit they would be entitled to before accepting the offer of a job. This fear of the unknown provides a substantial barrier to work.

So too does the amount of time taken to process new claims

and to calculate benefit entitlements after a change of circumstance. The existence of so many different benefits, each with a separate regulatory regime may make bureaucratic sense, but it makes absolutely no sense to claimants (Rowlingson and Newburn, 1997[1]). Indeed, the social security system may have contributed to the growth in welfare dependency, particularly amongst the older age groups. Some parts of the system still create work and savings disincentives. Eligibility requirements for many income support payments are still focused primarily on incapacity and barriers to work, rather than emphasising people's capacities and potential.

In short, the income support system still does too little to prevent and discourage welfare dependency. Under the current arrangements, taxpayers and benefits recipients are set against one another; the systems are split apart and do not treat people equally.

If the system works as it should, those in receipt of benefit now will pay tax in the future (in fact anyone who buys anything is already a VAT taxpayer). Moreover, with the rise of in-work benefits the majority of taxpayers are also benefit recipients. We all receive 'benefits' from universal services such as health and education. The approach demonstrates that with a sufficiently open mind a system of tax and benefits, which is both fair and which avoids creating personal and financial hardship through unemployment and poverty traps, can be developed.

As policies currently stand, people who are offered casual or short-term work may be unwilling to declare it to the Benefits Agency for fear of losing their benefits immediately. Similarly, people may be forced to refuse offers of work. This will be the case if the additional costs associated with working (e.g. travel) added to the amount of benefit lost is greater than their take-home pay. Under a basic income system, which recognises citizenship and participation, individuals would be able to take-up casual work when it was on offer and to see the immediate benefit of their labour. It would also allow people who can not guarantee their hours of work every week (those with caring responsibilities or some disabled people for example) to do as much as they can and still benefit. This system has an in-built incentive to work (it avoids the unemployment trap) and does not penalise people for being honest. Above all, this system treats benefits recipients and tax-payers in the same way. Neither group is assumed to have a monopoly of honesty and the sharp division between those who always receive, and those who always give, is eroded.

The approach also recognises the benefits of empowering the citizen in an active society and economy. It recognises that power is concerned with people's ability to achieve what they aim to do; and that empowerment is concerned with the processes which assist them to do so. It also emphasises the fact that the concept of empowerment spans both the individual and collective.

Social and economic support systems should be concerned with power 'TO' and not with power 'OVER'. A social support system's power 'TO' is concerned simply with the system's ability to act, and implicit in being able to act is the ability to define purpose and the means of achievement and evaluation (Little, 2000²). It is virtually impossible to be confident about either purpose or means except by reference to a system of values. In the absence of a value system the discussion about means and ends tends to go round in circles. Therefore, limits to power are important to discuss within the profile of the tax/benefit system. Here the concern should be about enabling choices and facilitating action to achieve them. Inevitably, there needs to be a recognition of constraints: delineating constraints and deciding what to do about them is an essential part of the social protection system (Beck, 1992).

Steps towards a basic income scheme

I am guided by the core concern of developing an income distribution system that would ensure every person in society had sufficient income to live life with dignity. This is a core justice issue that is not given appropriate priority in most economic and political arenas. A basic income approach addresses the huge changes emerging in the labour market and recognises the critical distinction between work and employment. Too often, modern economic and political thinking tends to equate these two concepts and see them as identical. However, it is clear that very large numbers of people are doing a great amount of work every day and this work is not recognised as employment. One consequence of this approach is that much work is not valued as an essential component of the progress of society.

Introducing a basic income system would demand huge transformation in social, economic, political and cultural terrain. The need for integrating the tax and welfare systems has been widely acknowledged for a number of decades. In the last few years there have been a number of very interesting and useful developments in this area. These include:

- The introduction of a tax credits systems;
- The use of tax credits to make payments to stay-at-home spouses with caring duties;
- The commissioning of a number of studies on economic value of social participation; and
- The developing dialogue on social enterprise.

What we are witnessing here is a very vibrant, ongoing debate about the shape and integration of the tax and welfare systems.

Movement in the direction of a basic income scheme takes the progressive elements of existing tax credit systems whilst tackling the flaws. Equity between the low-paid and better off would require not only that the value of tax credits be increased but also that tax credits be made 'refundable'. When the tax credit is not refundable those with incomes so low that their tax bill is lower than the value of the tax credit do not benefit from any increase in the value of that tax credit. When tax credits are refundable, those whose tax bills are less than the credit receive a payment equal to the difference. The main beneficiaries of refundable tax credits would be low-paid employees.

The major advantage of making tax credits refundable would be in addressing the disincentives currently associated with low paid employment. If refundable tax credits were introduced, subsequent increases in the level of the tax credit would then be of equal value to all employees.

With a refundable tax credit system in place *every adult with a job* would, in effect, gain the full value of a tax credit. Almost every other adult in the country i.e. *adults without a job*, are entitled to a social welfare payment. All that is required is to designate a part of the social welfare payment equivalent to the tax credit, as a tax credit, and reduce the social welfare payment accordingly. Then we have a situation where everyone has an effective tax credit. The simplest way to administer this refundable tax credit system would be to pay it as a basic income.

Every child in the country already has a tax-free child benefit payment paid to its parents or carers. This, in effect, is a basic income. Consequently, the path currently being followed in the UK could be transformed, rather easily, into a basic income system.

Advocating basic income on other fronts

Although the arguments from welfare effectiveness is strong, in the ongoing discussions and advocacy of basic income it is important to keep in mind that work is required on different fronts. The *economics* of basic income must be constantly assessed. This has both macro and micro dimensions – ranging from its impact on the labour market or migration patterns to the levels at which payments are made and the tax rate it requires or the tax base on which it is to be developed.[3] Work at this level is fundamental and must be constantly pursued, otherwise the argument may be lost because its viability in economic terms may not be obvious at first glance. The issue of adequacy is crucial, consequently the level at which the basic income payments are set for adults and children need not be very high but should be sufficient to enable people live life with basic dignity.

The *cultural* arguments for basic income also require constant attention. This dimension is crucial because the economic arguments may be won but the political system may reject the introduction of a basic income system because it is perceived as being at odds with values such as efficiency, personal responsibility, participation, etc. The basic income supports each of these values. It also supports a range of other values that are considered as important in much of the debate about the core culture of a modern society: rights, responsibility, guardianship and stewardship.

The *social* dimension of introducing a basic income system must also be pursued. Some have argued against it because it would create new exclusions. Others have suggested that it would allow the lazy to benefit at the expense of others. The issue of adequacy arises again. If the payments levels are too low they will not ensure that everyone has sufficient income to live life with basic dignity. If this were to happen then the basic income system would fail to meet the requirements of at least one of the guiding principles which should guide any tax/welfare system.

While basic income may be among social policies that implement principles of economic justice, we cannot rule out (re)distributive policies of wage subsidisation, or more generally a *mix of basic income and wage subsidies*.[4] The task of a social democratic government includes making choices of an ethical nature on behalf of the governed, choices that are conditions of the good life for individuals.[5]

Social justice

The idea of an active welfare state, which adopts increased participation as a central goal of social policy, should also be based upon a conception of social justice. To understand what this last requirement means, it is helpful to refer to a recent interpretation of the ideal of 'equality of opportunity' (see, e.g. Cohen 1989[a]; 1999[b], Roemer, 1996[c]). On this interpretation, equality of opportunity aims to redress the disadvantages people suffer through no fault of their own. More precisely, equality of opportunity aims to compensate individuals for factors that adversely affect their well-being, and for which they cannot reasonably be held responsible, because those factors are held to be beyond any individual's own span of control. The 'egalitarianism' aims to either *equalise* the impact of these 'factors' on people's well-being, or, alternatively, and less radically, to make those who are worst off, as well-off as is possible.

The criterion of the justice of participation means comprehensive opportunities for individuals to choose their own patterns of work, their own life-style, without having to fit into a vast array of standards. Gainful employment is of fundamental importance in the choice of a self-determined life-style, so that exclusion from gainful employment is tantamount to a refusal of elementary rights in participation.[9] Justice in participation is, however, not realised by access to gainful employment alone. Other areas of activity – from work in education and in the home, to social and civic involvement and to being self-employed – all of these should open up broad opportunities for participation. Therefore, we need conditions in society that can help to overcome the de facto one-sided – and particularly gender-specific – allocation of roles and activities.

A strategy of redistribution of work as a means against unemployment contains the beginnings for a more just society in respect of work. Such a strategy helps to upgrade gainful employment for women both in quantity and quality to form a base for an independent existence, and it replaces the standard model of the man as breadwinner. It opens the chance to create more quality time and it eases the transition to an activities-orientated society where activities other than gainful employment are fully integrated rather than downgraded at women's expense.

Another consideration is the possible effect the proposal for linking a basic income to a small income from gainful employment might have on social policies and policies for the labour market. A system for social security that is increasingly detached from gainful employment can offer a secure basic existence, which might make many jobs with minimal contractual commitments appealing to some groups of the population because the threatening phenomenon of the 'working poor' would be removed.[10] A basic income could open up the chance to organise forms of precarious employment, which would be more socially acceptable and more personally attractive – whether as part-time work, or as minimum employment. A basic income system would in effect increase the wage bargaining power of the worker. However, we need to emphasise the social importance of citizenship by making available an appropriate social infrastructure. This would include the clear affirmation that it is not a matter of compensation for denied gainful employment, but much more one of complementing this to allow citizens to realise their personal interest in the democratic life of the community.

From 'work pays' to 'benefit works' – critique and reform of existing policy

There is a need to develop policies and strategies that strike a better balance between providing a strong safety net and allowing all to participate fully in the workforce where they are able.

Government policy encouraging economic participation has in the past been on two main fronts. On one hand, assistance has been provided on a voluntary basis to some groups likely to benefit from investment in work-related skills (for instance lone parents). On the other hand, activity tests are applied stringently to ensure those able to work are actively pursuing employment opportunities.

More recently, the focus has turned to more active forms of assistance. The Government is interested in different approaches to increasing social and economic participation among income support recipients and those at risk of long term dependency in the future. Its aims are to increase levels of economic and social participation among people who are at risk of long-term reliance on income support and who may benefit from earlier access to services or alternative approaches to building their capacities for participation. Each of these interventions will involve a face to face interview, referral to existing services where appropriate and development of a 'participation' plan, through a Social Enterprise Strategy. This approach may offer a cost-effective way of empowering recipients to identify their own pathways out of welfare. There is a need to overhaul the whole welfare system (both income support and services) and refocus it on participation. We need to reject approaches based on restricting access to payments or time limits for eligibility, while acknowledging that the poverty alleviation goal of the social safety net may have been over-emphasised and that the current system was failing many of those it had been designed to help, because there had been insufficient emphasis on welfare to participation. A new architecture for a social support system should activate, enhance and support people's capacities for economic and social participation (Jordan et al, 2000)[11]. Particular problems with the current system included:

- Fragmented service delivery arrangements which are not sufficiently focused on participation goals for all people of workforce age;
- A rigid, categorical and complex array of payments which relies heavily on presumptions of capacity for participation and doesn't recognise the diversity of each individual's capacity and circumstances;
- Poor incentives and support for some forms of work;
- Insufficient recognition of the many forms in which people make a contribution, including social participation.

Welfare reform is a community wide issue that needs commitment from business and the broader community as well as government in order to be successful. A long term vision for a new participation support system is developing, which includes the following five key features:

- Individualised service delivery
- Simpler income support structure
- Incentives and financial assistance
- Mutual Obligation
- Social Partnership

Each of these features required attention both to achieve balance between additional facilitation, incentives and requirement, and to maximise the likely outcomes of welfare to work or welfare to participate initiatives.

An individualised service delivery approach would focus on individual capacities and outcomes, rather than payment category, when determining access to services and assistance. The new service delivery system would link the disparate parts of the current service delivery network through a central gateway for assessment and streaming, backed up with integrated communications and information technology management and reporting systems. Streaming to one of three levels of service provision would depend upon a person's assessed labour force disadvantage or barrier to participation and likely risk of long term dependence, along with the likelihood of achieving an outcome.

This system would require much more sophisticated assessment and profiling tools than are currently available. It is estimated that around 75 per cent of people would be referred to the base level of assistance that offered self-help and information provision. Typically people in this tier would include those who are job ready or participating in education and need no specific assistance, those who are caring or parenting and not yet ready for economic participation and those for whom an outcome is considered remote.

The second tier is tilted towards low-level brokerage and would encompass those people who need to be linked to available service or require additional help with planning.

The most intensive tier – high-level brokerage – would offer individualised assistance to those who are not yet ready for participation or who have multiple barriers to assistance but for whom an outcome is considered likely with the provision of such assistance.

A diagram of this conceptual model of the service delivery system is given below:

Figure 4.1
Individualised services

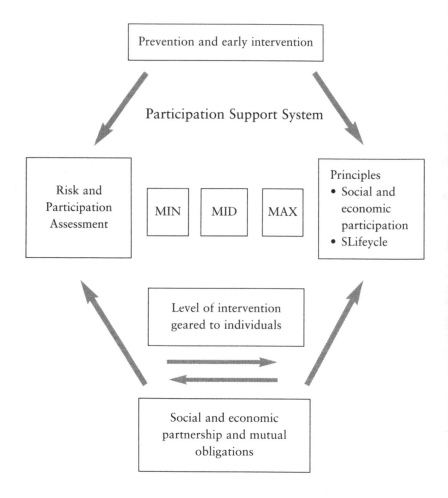

This translates into a new architecture for service delivery, as given below:

Figure 4.2
Proposed Delivery Service

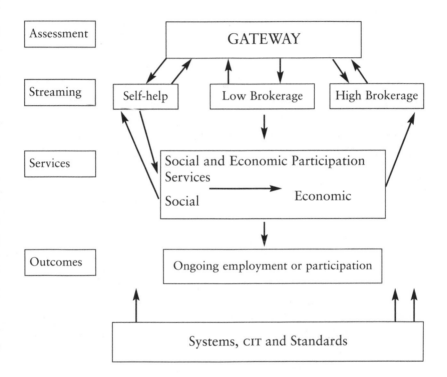

The challenges for government thrown up by this model include:

- The development of better assessment and profiling tools to aid streaming and rationing of services;
- Determining likely outcomes for people with more complex needs;
- Incorporating access to social participation opportunities (e.g. volunteer work) within the model;

- Providing a degree of integration across disparate providers and agencies;
- Determining appropriate funding regimes – input, output or outcome based;
- Privacy concerns with more integration of ICT networks;
- Identifying agencies best placed to carry out the roles of gateway, low level broker and high level broker; and
- Appropriate risk management and assurance frameworks.

There are a number of shortcomings with the current categorical system of income support available to people of workforce age. In particular the system does not adequately recognise the individual variation in circumstances and capacity among people receiving income support nor does it support the transitions that people make across their life course, for example, from being a primary carer back into the labour market. Within the current system there can be identified some unintended behavioural incentives, including incentives to reduce work effort in order to meet eligibility rules for more generous pensions and/or non-activity tested allowances (such as the Working Families Tax Credit). Complexity of the arrangements is creating confusion for staff administering the system as well as claimants.

In the longer term, the categorical system of pensions and allowances should be replaced with an integrated payment structure for all people. The nature of this payment structure would be a conditional minimum income (or participation income) model with a base rate and supplementary add-on modules to address various additional needs such as:

- The costs of children
- The additional cost of living as the only adult in a household
- Additional costs of a lone parent or single income family
- Costs of childcare
- Housing costs above some specified level
- Costs of disability
- Remote area costs

In addition to these forms of support, a participation supplement is also suggested as either a fortnightly payment (which could build up as a lump sum in an 'account') to address the additional costs of some forms of economic participation (e.g. education, voluntary work, etc.).

It is also proposed to adopt a consistent approach to indexing and taxation treatment of workforce age payments. The long-term nature of this goal is highlighted by the likely costs involved and the difficult balance government would need to consider in implementing a more integrated payment structure. In addition, the issue of coverage arises because at present full-time workers and the self-employed are generally excluded from receiving unemployment payments because of their inability to meet the test of seeking and being available for suitable paid work. Removal of sharp distinctions between the 'unemployed' and other participants as a basis for payment would bring this issue to the fore.

Social partners in a new infrastructure

A very broad notion of mutual obligations is required. Within this model, government, business, communities, non-government organisations and individuals should be seen as having social obligations to society at large. Each of these has a role to play in enabling people to move from welfare to participation (and work) and additional efforts would be needed from each to implement welfare reform.

Credit unions would allow income support recipients with seasonal or intermittent casual work to build up a 'bank' of unused income, test free. Once they undertake work, their income is offset against this credit until the balance is reduced to nil thus evening out the impact of income tests on intermittent earnings. If extended to people who return to permanent full-time work, the credit union could also act as a return to work bonus by providing income support for a short period (one or two weeks) after a person has returned to work (Duffin, forthcoming).[12]

Nonetheless, we need to differentiate between obligations that are societal expectations and those that are requirements, enshrined in legislation. Strategies for achieving voluntary compliance from each of these parties must be seen as important with sanctions only to be used as a last resort. The government's obligations can be summarised as managing the economy; maintaining a strong social safety net; managing social risk; investing in individual and community capacity building; and expanding its leadership role in providing opportunities for disadvantaged people and thus (re) establishing a social and economic contract between the elected and the electorate.

Additional effort from business is needed in providing employment opportunities for people who experience discrimination, including people from minority ethnic backgrounds, mature age workers, people with disabilities and workers with family responsibilities. In addition the notion of corporate social responsibility is an area for further development.

Communities have an important role in tackling social and economic exclusion within a social capital building. Particularly disadvantaged communities in depressed regions need additional support from government to tackle joblessness and create opportunities for participation.

Finally, a framework of mutual obligations could encompass all people of workforce age receiving income support. Within this framework, people with the capacity and availability would be expected to undertake some form of economic participation with a return to work goal. Others with substantial caring responsibilities or with permanent incapacity would not be required to participate economically but their social participation would be seen as discharging their mutual obligation. In some circumstances it is envisaged that people could choose social participation as a substitute for economic participation or as a pathway towards economic participation (e.g. voluntary work) but they would not be required to undertake social participation for its own sake (e.g. workfare programmes). The fundamental approach taken to mutual obligation is to tailor requirements (if any) to a person's specific individual capacities and circumstances within the context of their community and family.

There is widespread support for such an approach from a range of constituencies in the UK. There is evidence of wide community support for appropriate forms of participation as the basis of income support receipt for those with capacity (Lewis, 2000)[13]. It is also important to note that income support recipients generally wish to participate themselves.

Social and economic partners are a key to the delivery of this new architecture for welfare. These partnerships are an important strategy for building the capacity of communities to solve their own problems and provide greater opportunities for economic and social participation. This is especially important in regions of concentrated disadvantage and joblessness.

Four important processes in community capacity building can be identified:

- Community economic development;
- Community-enterprise partnerships;
- Social entrepreneurship; and
- Fostering micro-business.

The emphasis on social partnerships and the community level domain is influenced by their belief that strong stocks of social capital can counter social and economic exclusion and provide additional resources to disadvantaged communities and individuals. In addition, there is a need to invest both at the community and individual level and the benefits of social participation for building individual's capacities for participation. Social entrepreneurship, community business partnerships and micro-business are all seen as means of increasing the available opportunities for social and economic participation.

These strategies are particularly important for people from minority ethnic backgrounds, young people and those at great risk of marginalisation from economic and social life. The way forward for a new architecture for welfare, which recognises citizenship, can be mapped out. It acknowledges the need for more research, modelling and evaluation before full-scale implementation of a social and economic participation support system. It also identifies some of the difficult choices government will confront in refining its welfare to work policy approach.

The welfare reform process in the UK appears to have galvanised community opinion that the current system is too passive and should seek to activate participation among people on welfare rather than leaving the issue of when and whether to participate up to individual recipients. The government wishes to provide ways of assisting people who are disadvantaged that strike a better balance between its ongoing commitment to maintain a strong safety net and its responsibility to develop policies and strategies allowing all to participate fully where they are able. Six principles of a social and economic participation can be matched with New Labour's welfare agenda. These are:

- Maintaining equity, simplicity, transparency and sustainability;
- Establishing better incentives for people receiving social security payments, so that work, education, skill development and civic participation are rewarded;
- Creating greater opportunities for people to increase self-reliance and capacity-building, rather than merely providing a passive safety net;
- Expecting people on income support to help themselves and contribute to society through increased social and economic participation in a framework of Mutual Obligation;
- Providing choices and support for individuals and families with more tailored assistance that focuses on prevention and early intervention; and
- Maintaining the Government's disciplined approach to fiscal policy.

Currently, the tax and benefits system is unfair and traps people in poverty and unemployment. It is not possible to reform the system as it currently stands. It may be possible to reduce some of its worst aspects by tinkering with starting rates of tax and benefit tapers, but the inherent inequality in the way that tax-payers and benefits recipients are treated will remain. Policy-makers and politicians must take this opportunity to consider a total reconfiguring of the tax and benefits system – building on the start made with the Working Families Tax Credit. Without this, it is impossible to imagine that any changes will do more than transform an awful system into a bad one.

References

[1] Rowlingson, K and Newburn, T (1997) *Social security Fraud*, London, Policy Studies Institute.
[2] Little, R (2000), *A Balance of Power? In Contending Images of World Politics*, eds. Greg Fry and Jacinta O'Hagan, London, MacMillan.
[3] Ward, Sean (1998), 'Basic Income' in Sean Healy and Brigid Reynolds (eds.), *Social Policy in Ireland*, Dublin, Oak Tree Press.
[4] Honohan, Patrick (1987), 'A Radical Reform of Social Welfare and Income Tax Evaluated', *Administration*, Vol. 35, No. 1.
[5] Vandenbroucke, F (1998), 'European Social Democracy and the Third Way: Convergence, Divisions, and Shared Questions', paper presented at the conference 'Labour In Government: The Third Way and the Future of Social Democracy', Minda de Gunzburg Center for European Studies, Harvard University, 13-15th November 1998.
[6] Cohen, GA (1989), 'On the Currency of Egalitarian Justice', *Ethics* 99 (4), 906-44. (1993), 'Equality of What? On Welfare, Goods, and Capabilities', in: M Nussbaum and AK Sen, *The Quality of Life*, Oxford, Clarendon Press, 9-29.
[7] Cohen (1999), 'Socialism and Equality of Opportunity', in: M Rosen and J Wolff, *Political Thought*, Oxford University Press, 354-8.
[8] Roemer, JE, (1996b), 'On a Mechanism for Implementing Egalitarianism with Responsibility', in: F Farina, F Hahn, and S Vannucci (eds.), *Ethics, Rationality, and Economic Behaviour*, Oxford, Clarendon Press, 142-58.
[9] Von Parijs, Ph. (1995), *Real Freedom for All. What (if Anything) Can Justify Capitalism?* Oxford, Clarendon Press
[10] Topel, RH (1997), 'Factor Proportions and Relative Wages: The Supply-side Determinants of Wage Inequality', *Journal of Economic Perspectives* 11 (2), 55-74.
[11] Jordan, B, et al, (2000), Stumbling towards basic income: the prospects for tax-benefit integration, Scan, London
[12] Duffin, S, (forthcoming), Delivering economic empowerment, SINE, Edinburgh
[13] Lewis, J, (2000) *Unpaid care work is a bar to full employment*, British Association for the Advancement of Science's Festival of Science in London

5

Time and Money for
a Sustainable Economy

BARBARA MacLENNAN

Getting and spending, we lay waste our powers;
Little we see in Nature that is ours;
William Wordsworth, 1806

Two ways of moving towards a sustainable economy are explored
in this chapter. They involve breaking with certain kinds of
dependency and promoting an active political culture. Combined
with other economic policies, the proposals fit within a broader
approach that could include new political settlements and
international accords. The fundamental changes required in the
policies of the World Trade Organisation, the International
Monetary Fund and the World Bank involve daunting struggles
against powerful forces. While campaigning on the wider issues,
however, it is possible to influence more directly the economy of
everyday life. An individual initiative taken further by people
acting together could lead to changes in political culture involving
less dependence on changes from above. This is not to
underestimate the importance of government action and statutory
reform but to combat feelings of powerlessness, apathy and
hopelessness and encourage, instead, the feeling that something
can be done and much can be achieved.

Both time and money spent organising the provision of
swimming pools, crèches, community centres, street gardens and
playgrounds would modify the commercialisation of social life.
Allocating less time to the business sector of the economy and
more time to the community and household sectors would tend to
use up fewer resources. Though, historically, public projects may

have caused as much environmental damage as the projects of capitalist private enterprise, it is only in the latter that there is actually an incentive for built-in obsolescence to replace an old model with the new. Community investment would require more building materials; the demand for some trades – plumbers, heating engineers and architects – would rise; but fewer commodities would be consumed.

Consumer culture targets women especially, to persuade them that shopping is a satisfying way of spending free time. While time and money are linked in various ways, the focus of this chapter is on money in the sense of finance for investment, which yields benefits over time into the future.

Power to influence the future of the economy lies with those who take investment decisions. Crucial for their implementation is the availability of finance. In neither the business sector nor the public sector where funds may be raised by borrowing, or, alternatively, may be drawn from undistributed profits or tax revenue, do women have much influence on investment decisions. Conversely, in community associations where they may have more influence, almost no finance for investment is obtainable. The government in Norway has ordered firms to ensure that at least 40% of their board members are women; this compares with only 2% in the boardrooms of UK firms quoted on the stock exchange. Reform of company law is one way of redressing the gender imbalance in power to influence the future. Another is the possibility of reallocating bank credit to bring about structural change, involving also a change in the balance between consumption and investment. Commercial banks create new money in the form of loans and this gives the economy flexibility to develop in new directions. Redistributing bank credit from personal loans for car purchase and cosmetic surgery to the finance of community projects would change the pattern of demand and consequently the composition of output. This chapter surveys the prospects for developing a better-balanced economy through changes in the allocation of bank credit.

In the following section, structural change, often cited as

desirable, is defined in a distinctive way. Next, I review the range of policies available to reduce hours of full-time employment and to negotiate, at the same time, a redistribution of work in the home. Then, I put forward proposals to change banking practice and obtain finance for community investment. Finally, I will consider the wider prospects for the Scottish economy. Throughout, I wish to emphasise the opportunities for addressing problems by different means to suit the varying circumstances and volition of assorted groups and individuals.

Economic and social structure

Though all national economies can be described as mixed economies, their structural characteristics will differ in the relative levels of activity taking place in business, in the public sector, in the voluntary sector and in households. They will also differ as regards the composition of national output: the amounts of food, drink, textiles, building materials, machine tools, policing, stock-broking and care provided within the economy. An idea of the size of each sector can be gained from the aggregate number of hours worked per annum in the household sector as compared to the number of hours worked in the public sector, in the business sector and in the voluntary sector[1].

However much the business model has come to permeate all other sectors, a distinct ethos with distinct social relations survives within each. Social relations in the household, though they may resemble them in some respects, are distinguishable from relations of production in capitalist businesses: physical and emotional bonds are closer and more intense; food is produced not for profit but to be eaten; no wages are received for the work done; the ownership of the means of production is different. Likewise, social relations within the public sector are still qualitatively distinct though perhaps increasingly similar to capitalist relations: they too are hierarchical; but different forms of personal ambition vie with the ethos of public service and the norms of capitalist efficiency. Motivations within voluntary organisations too are still distinguishable from those in business. All sectors are linked together, reproducing through time an ever-changing economic and social structure.

Whether conducted by individual entrepreneurs, by public companies with limited liability, or by multinational corporations, a great deal of the dynamic of social change comes from the convulsive expansion of capitalist production. Capitalism sets the tone of much of economic, social and political life, permeating and interacting with patriarchal gender relations. But unequal relations between men and women, like other kinds of subordination, can in themselves foster resistance and lead to change. I regard gender relations, therefore, as being not only intrinsic to economic and social structure but also capable of transforming it.

It is within the social setting of the household that new people are created and have their first formative experience of life, with decisive consequences for their future and the relationships that will constitute their society. Economic policies that favour business and trade over the household distort the economy and society. The wellbeing of households depends not only on what is happening, or not happening, within them, but also on the economic, social and natural environment. Because all are linked together, it is affected by what is happening in the other sectors, by the excesses of business and the deficiencies of community. The economic and social structure, envisaged as what people create, what they do, and with whom they do it, is as critical for sustainability as it is important for human welfare and for the evolution of the culture.

Time

The following proposals relating to time and money are directed towards improving the quality of social relations, in general, and their sustainability across generations, in particular. Women in Scotland are producing fewer children than women in the rest of the UK; the birth rate is below replacement rate generating an ageing population; the Scottish population is not being sustained. Though a social compulsion to have children can be oppressive, socio-economic conditions that prevent anyone from having children break the continuity linking each person to past generations and to the future. Individuals are deprived of a place in human history. Over fifty per cent of women in the professions and in the upper echelons of management are childless[2]. It is open to any such woman to use the right to family life, guaranteed by the European Convention, to mount a legal challenge against working hours and conditions, against intensity of work and the stress of working in an atmosphere in which no life outside work is acknowledged. No one has yet done this.

There are many other ways of confronting the long-hours culture. As reported in *Labour Market Trends*[3], almost 20% of employees would accept a lower income in return for shorter working hours. A smaller percentage is underemployed in the sense of wanting to work longer hours for more income. Though the scope should not be exaggerated, some limited redistribution of hours might be possible so that unemployed and underemployed people could take up hours of work that some of the over-employed would gladly relinquish. Men in the UK work longer hours than anywhere else in Europe; they also take fewer holidays.

Trade union negotiation for the sort of reduction in hours that will actually improve the lives of their members whose priorities may now be different from those of the past is the appropriate response to pressure from the political and industrial establishment for greater work flexibility. Reduction of hours in full-time employment would facilitate redistribution of work and thus redistribution of income between women and men – both unpaid work within the home, including the care of children and other dependants, and paid work in employment or other remunerated occupation. In Scotland, teachers and other groups have negotiated a shorter working week. More generally, however, trade unions have not given a sufficiently high priority to reduction in hours of full-time employment, despite widespread dissatisfaction over the difficulties of combining employment with work in the home. Within the context of decentralised bargaining over wages, conditions and productivity, there is much that can be done to strengthen an hours-of-work objective appropriate to a sustainable economy.

Consider a 25-hour week as a long-run objective. This would be compatible with family life and, for those not engaged in looking after dependents, would offer hours free for varied activity and enjoyment. Within such a policy perspective, particular productivity negotiations and pay bargaining would be crucial. Some groups, as mentioned above, will accept a reduction in income with a reduction in hours. In this case, there is no increase in wage costs to employers though there may be some increase in non-wage costs.

Lessons can be learned from the French initiative for a 35-hour week. For workers on low wages, including those dependent on overtime for their money income, reduction in hours cannot be allowed to reduce income. Reducing the working week from, say, 40 hours to 25 hours, specifically for those on the minimum wage, would require a compensating increase of the same proportion (i.e. 37½ per cent) in the hourly rate to maintain the same weekly income. Getting the same wages for fewer hours would, unless productivity increased pro rata, raise costs and therefore prices. Adopted as a long-run objective, however, the reduction in hours and increase in prices would take place little by little, spread over a number of years. As pointed out, more than two and a half centuries ago, by the Scottish philosopher, David Hume, gradually rising prices are good for profits; firms have an incentive to invest and so maintain employment. At times such as the present when the rate of inflation is below that which the monetary authorities, currently the Bank of England, are required to aim at, a reduction in hours of work would help achieve the target 2.5% per annum prices increase.

The negotiations, however, will be complex. With the decline in Scotland of coalmining, engineering, textiles, electronics, and now fishing, changed union membership has yet to be fully translated into changed union demands. Women want a shorter working day whereas men want a compressed working week, with a long weekend. On the other hand, employers who comply with shorter hours by extending the length of breaks during the day do not benefit workers. The most notorious instance is the zero-hours contract: young people in fast-food outlets are paid only for the minutes that they are actually making or serving food. Between-times, when there is no custom, they are not paid but have to be on the spot, not their own persons, alert but idle. Despite the complexity, an appropriate response to the rhetoric of flexibility[4] is nevertheless to be found in negotiating claims for both general and specific entitlements to shorter working hours.

Statutory arrangements have some role in effecting cultural change. Whereas, until recently, in the UK, there was a financial penalty for fathers taking time off, in Norway, there is a penalty for fathers not taking time off at the birth of a child. Entitlement to the full grant available in Norway when a child is born depends upon the father of the child taking leave from his paid work. In the UK, by contrast, the right of fathers since 1999 to take three weeks unpaid parental leave, though better than no right at all, involved loss of income at the time of a child's birth. A Bill coming into effect in 2003 proposes two weeks paid paternity leave for which an estimated 450,000 fathers in the UK would be eligible each year. They can take leave in blocks of one or two weeks within 56 days of the birth or adoption of a child. At present, however, when nearly two thirds of firms already offer paternity leave, most fathers do not take it. Will converting it to a statutory right increase take-up? The trouble seems to be not so much that men do not want to take their entitlement but that work place culture prevents them from taking it.

The cultural icon, caring father and brilliant performer footballer David Beckham, emerging from a sport with a macho reputation, now organised on a capitalist basis, suggests that the image of masculinity may be undergoing change. That men still fear to appear un-masculine, however, indicates that the change is not sufficiently pervasive in the workforce or among managers.

The UK employment bill giving working mothers and fathers with children under the age of six, the right to ask for changes to their hours of work may fail for similar reasons. Although employment law accords the family recognition that was lacking before, both men and women still fear detriment to their careers from appearing uncommitted. Employees would prefer flexible hours to the company cars and leisure club membership offered, as perquisites, by management. Statutory change has limited effect while attitudes and practices, outside, to a large extent determine what is possible within the household.

In the micro-politics of resistance, conditions that make life unsustainable can be challenged in law, in workplace consultation or in the home, to re-negotiate the gender division of labour.

Money

The wellbeing of households depends not only on the amount of finance available to them but on the amounts distributed to other sectors of the economy. A change in banking custom and practice would enable community initiatives to make good failures of central and local government by providing finance for investment in sectors of the economy starved of funds and with no access to credit. Rebalancing the economic and social structure by providing substantial loans for community projects, as opposed to small loans for individuals, would moderate somewhat the convulsive expansion of capitalism and benefit the household sector.

Time and money are involved in the process of investment. Though a hard and fast definition of investment may not be possible, failure to distinguish between current expenditure and investment expenditure in the public sector promotes confusion that is not conducive to honest debate. Politicians tend to talk indiscriminately about investment in public services thus giving an impression of solidity, or prudence that would not attach to the more profligate-sounding 'expenditure'. Most health and education expenditure is not strictly speaking investment but rather current expenditure and, as such, should be financed from tax revenue. Investment, on the other hand, should be financed by borrowing, the rate of interest on which is lower for the public sector than for the business sector. This raises one of the most contentious issues of recent political debate.

The Scottish Executive following the path set by UK governments, both Conservative and New Labour, appears to believe that the higher cost of borrowing for the private sector is offset by efficiencies of business management and working practices. There is now a substantial volume of analysis of Public-Private Partnerships or Private Finance Initiatives, to challenge this belief, including the Accounts Commission for Scotland Audit Review, June 2002[5]. There has been no debate, however, about a possibility of transferring risk specifically to the commercial banks, while allowing for the expression of community initiative, democratic enthusiasm, and exuberant rage at the surroundings and conditions in which some people are obliged to live. It is a cause for celebration that there is no lack of community commitment among people living in the worst of neighbourhoods.

Any individual or collective application for a bank loan to finance a project that would manifestly make a great difference to a locality might be successful. Mindful of corporate social responsibility, a bank might agree to lend for such an undertaking. The story of such a success could generate others. Even the story that funds for such a project were refused would, in itself, contribute to the political argument in favour of change. Though an act of parliament could establish the idea of bank funding for community investment, change might also be instigated bit by bit through individual or collective action, without legislation. Banking culture can change with or without statutory compulsion. Though the passage of legislation may publicise new possibilities for community borrowing and so nourish ideas for projects stymied by lack of funds, local arrangements negotiated with local banks may, in the long run, be better adapted to needs, provided that the story of their success is broadcast to spread the word to other communities. Such a scheme is already in progress. In Wester Hailes, Edinburgh, a community previously ignored by banks, the representative council pointed out that the local population, despite poverty, collectively has a sizeable annual income, with the result that basic bank accounts and small loans for the start-up of individual businesses are now on offer. The bank with which the representative council negotiates, having had its attention drawn also to the substantial financial turnover and assets belonging to local voluntary organisations, is now keen to lend where there is a guaranteed stream of income. The next step is to get loans for projects where the expected stream of income is less certain. Would it expedite matters to have legislation that obliged the banks to lend for community projects?

The issue is not whether there should be bank regulation. This is accepted as necessary by banks themselves and by everyone else. Commercial banks create money through lending. In Scotland, the Bank of Scotland, the Royal Bank of Scotland and the Clydesdale Bank can still literarily print money. More usually, banks enter figures on balance sheets to allow borrowers to draw from them. Everywhere, banks are regulated to prevent them from lending or printing so much that they would not be able to repay those who deposit money with them and, from time to time, wish to make withdrawals. If they were not able to meet the withdrawals of depositors, banks would fail, as happened in Scotland throughout the 18th and 19th centuries. The prime object of regulation, therefore, is to avoid bank failure because this has disastrous economic consequences for all who use bank money. Customers lose their deposits; they cannot carry out transactions, the demand for goods and services falls, unemployment rises, people's incomes drop, and the economy virtually collapses. This is what regulation prevents.

Regulation clearly has advantages for the banks. As bank failure has become relatively rare, confidence in the banks has grown and the business of banking has burgeoned. At the level of the European Union, though there is a Single Banking Act, regulation remains the responsibility of individual states.

The issue, then, is what sort of bank regulation there should be. Over the last century and particularly in the last decade, there have been many mergers. Creating money is a profitable business and since 1991, when the UK government imposed a windfall tax on banks' profits, there has been recurrent speculation that such a levy might be imposed again as, for example, when record profits were announced in the summer of 2000. It proved, that time, to be a false alarm. Next, a report from the Competition Commission in October 2001 found the banks operating as a complex cartel making excess profits from small businesses. Amid renewed speculation of a windfall tax, the Chancellor of the Exchequer instead obliged the Royal Bank of Scotland, Lloyds TSB, Barclays, and HSBC, in their banking operations south of the border, either to offer a rate of interest on small businesses' accounts or to allow them to make transactions free of charge. These requirements were not forced on the banks' Scottish operations because, though the Royal Bank of Scotland, together with HBOS and Clydesdale, were found to have operated against the public interest in some of their dealings with small firms, they had not, despite this, succeeded 'for the most part' in making excess profits. They were, consequently, spared the rules imposed in March 2002, the outcome being a divergence between bank regulation in Scotland and that in the rest of the UK. Since the latter is just the sort of detailed regulation disliked by banks, it may open the way for negotiating a different kind of regulation that could not only be more palatable to the banks but could also do more for communities.

Issues of finance could be simpler within the framework of a Community Re-investment Act. In the US, a raft of such legislation emerged from the civil rights movement in the mid 1970s. The banks' practice of 'red-lining' run-down inner cities areas, to cut the costs of processing separate loan applications, withheld finance from black people still living in these areas, evacuated by whites. The legislation, as amended from time to time, has been very effective in some ways though unsatisfactory in others. The challenge would be to review the American experience to see how a Community Re-investment Act could be remodelled to suit the needs of a sustainable economy in Scotland. Of course, the banks would protest. Assessing a community venture in the localities where they work would take bank employees longer than ticking boxes for automated credit scoring. Costs would rise. On the other hand, excess profits draw the attention of regulators and since Scotland's booming financial-services industry has grown at about 5.5% a year for the past five years, the banks might accede with good grace to an increase in costs which would reduce their profits, especially as these projects would give substance to their claims to 'corporate citizenship'. They could take credit for giving credit. Although banks do not like limitations, they do learn to live with changed regulatory regimes. Scottish banks, like other European banks operating in the US, already have experience of having to comply with a Community Re-investment Act.

The great advantage of using the commercial banks for community finance is that, despite branch closures associated with the mergers of recent years, bank branches are still quite widely distributed throughout the country. Bank employees coming to work in these branches inevitably have some local knowledge and would get the opportunity of acquiring more to enable them to assess projects put forward by the communities. Where there are no branches, as in some of the most deprived neighbourhoods, banks operating nearby would collectively have the responsibility for making loans.

That there is a deficiency in finance for the so-called third sector is evidently recognised in London. While acknowledging the value of financial intermediaries in funding community development, Sir Eddie George, governor of the Bank of England, charged the banks and the government to alleviate that deficiency having regard to self-interest as well as social responsibility. While rumours that associates of the Chancellor of the Exchequer favour a Community Reinvestment Act are still to be substantiated communities can, without further ado, test banks' commitment to community investment, by putting forward projects for funding. When, in 2001, Chancellor Gordon Brown visited Harlem, New York, regenerated by bank finance in the last 20 years, he said that we do regeneration differently in the UK. Though different, it is not necessarily a better way.

The plethora of measures involved is such as to be only too likely to dissipate enthusiasm for any project. There is a new community investment tax credit in selected areas. There is exemption from stamp duty and exemption from VAT on property reclamation. There is a venture development fund. There are regional grants for new innovative industries. It is unlikely that the sort of people who know about local needs and have the energy to do something about them will want to spend their time on the details of applying for these complex and changing pecuniary supports. There is also the financial intermediary, Social Investment Scotland, a loan fund launched in September 2001, currently processing applications and, after nine months, ready to release its first two loans. Social Investment Scotland takes on the cost of assessment for the banks, which supply the capital. A Community Reinvestment Act, by contrast, would establish a statutory presumption that banks make loans available for investment; and hundreds of branches could deal with hundreds of applications.

Let us consider the kind of investment that involves the construction of buildings that in their lifetime, would bring in some income and other benefits over a prolonged period of time into the future. A swimming pool or a crèche would come into this category. People expect to pay for the use of swimming pools. Evidently, they feel passionate about their value, primarily for children and young people, and are even prepared to risk prosecution demonstrating for their preservation. Problems have arisen in many towns and cities because of neglect and deficient expenditure on maintenance that would have kept the buildings in good order over the years. Local authority revenue has been capped and their right to issue bonds has been curtailed by central government since the late 1970s. In the case of a crèche, you may wonder how a loan could be repaid if financed by community borrowing. Some of the repayment would come from employed parents who can recover up to 70% of the costs of childcare from tax credit. As for the rest, the 'third sector' has ample experience of raising money by imaginative and unorthodox means.

Community need is not restricted to urban areas. Many people working in the countryside believe private wealth to be necessary to maintain rural employment and look after the land. They use this as an argument against land reform, for retaining vast inequalities of landed wealth. For the purchase and maintenance of income-earning assets however, neither private wealth nor public subsidy is required. Despite this, the parliamentary Bill allowing crofters to purchase fishing rights on their land, against the will of the landlord if necessary, authorises government subsidy from National Lottery funds. Since income can be derived from hiring out fishing rights, loans could be repaid. Policy on bank lending could be much more general, much less specific than a subsidy for the purpose of buying riverside land. My proposal is to make finance more generally available rather than arranging dedicated or designated funds for every single purpose. As well as small businesses, including crofting and farming, projects of community investment could be initiated and carried to completion, in due course repaying the loan by some means or other. Loans should be available for investment in all sectors of the economy with special attention to the community sector that has, up to now, been neglected by the banks.

Visions of the future

How might the above proposals regarding time and money fit into a vision of a sustainable economy for Scotland? We can answer this with bit of realism about where we are, and some healthy dreaming for the future.

Figures published in August 2002 showed a small reduction in economic output in the last quarter of 2001 and the first quarter of 2002. Although two successive quarters of reduced output constitute what economists define as recession, this is no reason to get agitated. It is all to the good if the slightly lower output uses up fewer material resources. Anyway, a one percent reduction over two quarters is well within margins of error. In the judicious voice of the *Economist*, 'it may be that because the growth figures understate the importance of financial services, they overstate the gloom'. The fabrication of growth figures is complex; statisticians agree their figures, at present, are skewed and hope to fix them in 2003. Meanwhile, these doom-laden data can be viewed with scepticism. By contrast, what happens to employment and unemployment is important because most people depend on jobs for their income. Employment, so far, has kept up reasonably well but the next eighteen months will be crucial: if the banks provide finance for starting up small businesses, and, even more, if they were to finance substantial community ventures generating employment, then a rise in unemployment could be prevented. We have, in the past, had growth as a result of labour-saving technological innovation without any increase in employment; we could be satisfied, in the future, with an increase in employment without growth.

The Scottish Executive rightly identifies structural change and cultural change as policy objectives. The nature of the required changes, however, demands greater elaboration and further debate. In response to the report of 'recession', enterprise minister, Iain Gray, mentioned structural change but did not refer to what people create, what they do, and with whom they do it, which is of such consequence for human wellbeing and for the evolution of the culture. The First Minister re-emphasised the need for cultural change. This is not just a matter of infusing children with entrepreneurial spirit. As outlined above, the attitudes and objectives of managers, trade unionists and others in the workplace must change if children are to be properly cared for and become confident adults. Talk of skills and productivity is all very well but we need change also in the culture of the commercial banks in order to finance community investment as well as indigenous business. This would reduce reliance on inward investment which, in the financial year 2001-2, fell dramatically from £1.7 billion to £270 million.

The objective of not being over-dependent on trade should

feature in the economic policy of every country, including Scotland. To grow more of our own food, to create beautiful surroundings, both buildings and landscape, for spiritual uplift, to resist the blandishments of advertising and refuse to be designated only as consumers, to target areas of deprivation for levelling up and at the same time allow the diversity that community investment would bring into being; these are all part of a possible vision of the future. Certainly, exports are required to exchange for imports but we can reduce imports and turn a more discriminating ear to calls for help from export-oriented business. When luxury cashmere knitwear became the object of a punitive tariff imposed by the US in one of its trade disputes with the EU, mills in the Borders closed. Scottish firms designing clothes and footwear instead for Scottish bodies, Scottish work, and Scottish weather would test the homily that there is no bad weather only inadequate clothing. We have the raw materials and some of the skills to fashion high quality leather, wool and viscose into beautiful garments[6]. In a relatively high-wage economy, this is business that would suit small indigenous firms. Buying the cheapest throwaway clothing from China leads to a throwaway culture that discards unwanted articles, refuse, litter, and waste to pollute our environment.

The different sectors of the Scottish economy: agriculture, fishing, manufacture, tourism, and finance, all require careful scrutiny. The need for food security within Europe has to be balanced by recognition that primary-producing countries need markets. But too great a dependence on the market generally, on export earnings or on cash crops, renders the life of the poor precarious. Historically, trade was most important for Scotland when Britain led the world in industrial development. It is time now to adapt to a changed situation because Scotland has become over-dependent on 'export-led growth' and foreign direct investment, latterly in the electronics industry. Both here and abroad, tourism can have destructive effects on indigenous culture. Scots, with a beautiful landscape and a vibrant modern culture producing sleek new buildings, could be happy to have visitors from abroad while avoiding the worst dangers of heritage and kilted kitsch. Aesthetic pollution, short of the life-threatening pollution of land and water, lowers the spirit. We could raise our spirits – not our glasses – by creating beautiful surroundings, constructing fine buildings and enhancing natural landscape. To reduce consumption of alcohol and other drugs, Czech astronomer, Jenik Hollan, advocates restoring the night sky with focussed lighting, not leaking upwards into the heavens but illuminating only what needs to be lit, enabling us to see again the stars and planets. He compares the marvel of the sky at night to falling in love, but more reliable! More prosaically, the reduction of light pollution would save energy and allow people to see the night sky that has given spiritual uplift to humans from pre-historic times throughout their history.

As war was said, by von Clausewitz, to be the pursuit of politics by other means so consumerism is the pursuit of happiness by other means. Becoming less dependent on commodities for satisfaction entails not drowning one's sorrows in drink but relying on friendship for solace, not taking prozac to relieve depression but performing drama to act out one's miseries, not hallucinating with LSD but transforming fantasy into film, not burgling people's houses for their goods to get an adrenaline rush but instead courting danger by abseiling or skateboarding. To substitute activities and friendships for commodities and substances involves realising our dreams by designing things, venting aggression in karate, relieving trauma by writing history, fiction, or poetry, revisiting one's earliest experiences by having children instead of having therapy, spewing out the garbage one has been fed by yelling on stage, composing dissonant music, relieving tension in dance. Produced commodities will always be needed but different products, different goods and different material objects. Lots of bricks or new construction materials using compacted straw to build the swimming pools and community theatres; lots of musical instruments, more skateboards and roller-blades will be wanted than before. This is part of what is meant by changing the economic and social structure and recognising the importance, for human wellbeing and for the evolution of the culture, of what people create, what they do, and with whom they do it.

References

[1] National Statistics leaflet: UK 2000 *Time Use Survey* includes time spent on household chores, on voluntary tasks, caring for others, gender differences in child care, activities of the unemployed, participation in leisure activities, the balance between work and leisure etc. www.statistics.gov.uk/timeuse www.data-archive.ac.uk gershuny@essex.ac.uk.

[2] Women question whether their lifestyles are sustainable. Those without children feel that their jobs are incompatible with having a family: they are more likely than men not to have children, *Gender and Restructuring: Managerial Roles and Identities in the Public Sector,* 2002, by Dr Annette Davies and Dr Robyn Thomas.

[3] August 2002.

[4] For example, as expressed by Prime Minister, Tony Blair, at the EU summit in Barcelona, March 2002.

[5] *Taking the Initiative, Using PFI contracts to renew council schools.*

[6] Even nettles can be woven into textiles!

Taking account of the future:
business and trade in a global economy

OSBERT LANCASTER

The changes I've witnessed since I became involved in the environmental movement in the early 90s are quite remarkable. There has been a significant shift in consciousness about the impact of human activity on the natural environment – global climate change is overwhelmingly accepted by policy makers and the public. It's widely recognised that natural resources, such as fisheries and forests, and the natural life support system itself, are under threat of catastrophic damage. These ideas are no longer the preserve of activists and obscure scientific committees.

Over the same period there has been an increasing convergence between social and environmental concerns. Sustainable development explicitly recognises that environmental improvements must go hand in hand with social equity, not just for the present, but also for the benefit of generations to come. The concept of environmental justice, highlighted in February 2002 by Jack McConnell, emphasises the political importance of integrating social and environmental concerns.

The mid 1990s saw the rise of awareness among businesses of the importance of environmental concerns. The number of companies adopting recognised environmental management systems increased, and environmental management increasingly became a normal aspect of doing business. The publication in 2002 of the European Commission Green Paper on Corporate Social Responsibility, and the establishment of the FTSE4Good Index are just two indicators of the increasing recognition that the business sector now gives social concerns. The new organisation for social responsibility in Scotland – Agenda – has held a number of successful events, that have brought together business people, politicians and campaigners to discuss frankly and realistically the common problems we all face. Even five years ago, these meetings would not have attracted such a diverse mix of participants. A coalition of UK NGOs are currently mobilising around a Private Members Bill in Westminster, which would make businesses accountable to stakeholders other than their shareholders.

Whatever one calls it – environmental and social justice, social responsibility, sustainable development – there is no doubt that the inter-related environmental and social issues are very much on the agenda in Scotland – the political agenda, the business agenda and activist agenda. That's not to say everyone agrees – neither on the analysis of the problem, the solutions we should be aiming for, nor the strategy for moving forward. Activists accuse business people of jumping on the sustainability bandwagon and trying to use it to 'greenwash' unethical practices; business people accuse activists of being naïve and unrealistic; the public look to politicians to show leadership on the sustainability agenda; while politicians claim they are unable to move in advance of public opinion.

This sort of disagreement is inevitable – it is a normal part of the process of social and political change. Despite the differences in emphasis and priorities, underlying this ferment is a shared understanding that did not exist ten years ago – environmental, social and economic conditions are inextricably inter-related and must considered together. At first sight it seems that, with more political commitment and a greater sense of urgency, we might perhaps be on track for a sustainable economy – an economy where economic success leads to widespread social wellbeing and a richer, more diverse environment.

In this paper I will explain why just 'trying harder' is not enough. First, I will describe how we – the rich 'North' – are benefiting at the expense of the poor 'South'. Then I will outline the structural reasons that make this inevitable without fundamental change. Finally I will argue that fundamental change, despite appearing almost impossible, is in fact achievable, and that Scotland can play a key role in championing these changes.

Exporting environmental damage

As a child in the early '70s I spent a few weekends counting lichens. Inspired by children's TV programme Blue Peter, I helped monitor air pollution. Across the UK, children like me recorded the distribution of different types of lichen – more lichens meant cleaner air. Despite living in rural Norfolk I didn't find many lichens – certainly not the big, hairy ones that could only live in clean air.

Now our air – in respect of sulphur dioxide at least – is much cleaner, and all sorts of lichens are widespread. Good news for British air quality, but bad news for Scandinavian forests as we built taller chimneys for our power stations and exported our pollution over the North Sea. Our sulphur dioxide fell on Scandinavia as dilute sulphuric acid – acid rain that significantly affected the growth of trees and the chemistry of soil and watercourses. Acid rain did not only affect the environment; it also had economic and social consequences for forestry, agriculture and fishing.

Since the UK's Clean Air Act of 1956 and through successive European Environmental Action Plans, we have controlled the amount of pollution emitted by industry in order to protect workers, communities and the natural environment. As far back as 1802, the first Factory Act, among other matters, restricted the hours worked by apprentices to no more than twelve per day between 6.00 am and 9.00 pm. Other legislation to protect people at work has followed, both in the UK, and later through European directives. Despite difficulties with implementation and compliance, national and European legislation has, on the whole, successfully reduced pollution and ensured better working conditions.

However, as we improve our environmental regulations and workplace legislation, many industries move their operations to the South where regulations are weaker, poorly enforced or nonexistent. Our children can't deliver papers before they are thirteen but we pedestrianise our city centres with granite setts quarried by bonded child labour in India. We set targets for packaging recycling, whilst mining bauxite for aluminium floods and poisons tracts of the Amazonian rainforest the size of small countries. Scotland's textile industry has all but disappeared and our clothes are too cheap to be worth repairing but the women textile workers in South East Asia who make them often suffer appallingly unsafe working conditions.

Maybe we will be able to eradicate poverty in Scotland and to protect Scotland's environment. Wendy Alexander wrote in the 2001 Scottish Executive paper *A Smart, Successful Scotland*, 'we can create a dynamic enterprising economy where opportunity is extended to all and no one is left out'. Our present economic, environmental and social strategies are based on making Scotland one of the winners – achieving our success, our clean environment, our quality of life, not just by ignoring the needs of others, but by actively making their situation worse. We need to face up to this fact – and the consequences.

Exporting environmental damage and human exploitation will rebound on us. It will not protect us from the effects of global climate change and other forms of cross border pollution. Armed conflicts around the world are intimately bound up with access to resources, especially oil, water and land. Poverty, hunger and violence, fuelled by envy, create conditions for the fundamentalism and desperation that leads to attacks on symbols of oppression by people who believe they have nothing to lose. The so-called 'War on Terrorism' will, in the long run, do little to protect us from the consequences.

Free trade – and not so free

Near Holyrood a billboard for Safeway proudly proclaims:

We've ground down the price of coffee.

Someone with a spray can and a conscience has added:

...and pushed millions of farmers into poverty.

It's not only the fact that we export our pollution and exploitation that causes problems for the poor countries of the South and destroys the environment. The national laws, taxation systems, regulations, international treaties, bilateral and multilateral trade agreements that uphold the system of 'free trade', are weighted against the poor and the environment.

This is nothing new; the Dutch and the British East India Companies in the 17th and 18th Centuries created immense wealth for their shareholders and revenues for the home countries through the expropriation of land and the exploitation of native people. Trade with the West Indies and North America, much of which paid for the building of Victorian Glasgow, was based on the labour of slaves. Grain farming in Australia and dairy farming in New Zealand destroyed eco-systems to feed Britain – mother of the Empire.

Of course, the economic success of the empires of 18th and 19th Centuries was not based on 'free trade'; it was based on monopolies and protectionism. Today the economic superpowers are calling for trade barriers to be knocked down, the end of protectionism, for every country to be given equal access to all markets – that's why the World Trade Organisation (wto) was established in 1995, to drive forward and to police these reforms. A cartoon from the time of the Uruguay Round of the General Agreement on Tariffs and Trade (GATT), the forerunner of the wto, summarises the objectives of liberalising trade: a powerful Western businessman towers over a wizened South American peasant as he explains: 'Of course it's fair, you can ride roughshod over our economy, and we can ride roughshod over yours'.

The cartoonist assumes that with a level playing field the rich economies will overwhelm the poor economies by sheer weight of resources. In fact it's more subtle than that. An Oxfam Briefing[1] demonstrates how Northern governments are having their cake and eating it – forcing open other countries markets, while keeping theirs as closed as possible. According to Oxfam 'the record of industrialised countries in the area of trade policy is one of heroic under-achievement. They have collectively reneged on every commitment made'.

- According to the United Nations' figures, unfair protectionist policies mean developing countries are losing around US$100bn every year;
- Rich countries favour other rich countries – tariff barriers are four times higher for poor countries than for industrialised countries;
- In direct breach of promises made, Northern countries have not reduced agricultural subsidies, but have increased them to US$350bn a year;
- Rich countries promised to phase out restrictions on one of the developing world's most important manufactured exports – textiles and garments – but have failed to fulfil this commitment.

In a closely run competition the United States and the European Union have been declared joint winners in the Oxfam's Double Standards league.[2] The Common Agricultural Policy is just one of the most visible of the EU's double standards. While calling on poor countries to open markets and abolish subsidies, CAP subsidies depress and destabilise markets worldwide, destroying smallholders' livelihoods throughout the developing world. European sugar-production costs, for example, are among the world's highest. But, by setting domestic sugar prices at three times international prices, and subsidising the export of excess production, the EU is the world's second biggest sugar exporter. EU consumers pay €1.6bn for the privilege of blocking poor countries like Mozambique from European markets, depressing world prices and so reducing the foreign exchange earnings of low cost producers such as Brazil, Thailand and Southern Africa.

Stephen Byers MP, former UK Secretary of State for Trade and Industry, recently returned from a visit to Africa saying, 'The reality is that in the majority of cases wholesale liberalisation coupled with reliance on market forces simply hasn't worked'. It's bizarre therefore that the rich countries are arguing that poor countries will benefit from the next round of trade 'liberalisation' – trade in services. The General Agreement on Trade in Services (GATS, not to be confused with the earlier GATT), will extend WTO rules to services – including banking, waste management, health services, education and retailing.

The World Development Movement report *Out of Service* [4] highlights two dangers of GATS. Firstly, the provision of services is a highly political issue, and integral to all economies and societies. The provision of basic services such as health care, sanitation, power, and education are part of the responsibility of governments, and cannot be left to the market alone. Secondly, GATS rules will extend deeper into all government's domestic decision making than many other trade agreements – they have a profound effect on government's ability to govern. If implemented GATS will irreversibly undermine the potential of all governments to control or direct economic development, and to implement policies to protect the poor and the environment. Theoretically GATS will apply to all nations – if previous experience is anything to go by, the Northern countries will successfully avoid implementing aspects that puts them at a disadvantage while forcing the South to implement in full.

Byers' statement – 'wholesale liberalisation coupled with reliance on market forces simply hasn't worked' [5] – is deeply ironic. There has not been 'wholesale' liberalisation, but unequal liberalisation which has favoured the rich at the expense of the poor; the 'market' has operated within a rigged system where smallholders in the South compete with subsidised and protected agri-businesses in the North. In the 1980s the Thatcher economy was great if you were one of the winners – for the losers it was hell. Wealth did not 'trickle down' then – and globally it's not trickling down now. Whatever the intellectual and political justifications, the whole structure of international trade, including WTO and GATS, is in practice based on sucking wealth up, from the poor countries to countries to the rich.

International trade, in its present form at least, is not contributing to social justice. We in Scotland might end up better off; we might reduce Scottish inequity and poverty. But we will be doing this on the back of poor countries in other parts of the world. But international trade is not only sucking wealth from the South – Northern countries are using resources and producing carbon dioxide at many times the level which is sustainable – and has been for decades. Friends of the Earth has highlighted this in their 'ecological debt' campaign[5], and argue that the North has an obligation, not only to reduce its consumption, but to recompense Southern countries for their past exploitation. There is a strong moral message here – we should not over-consume resources at the expense of others. But there is also a strong element of self-interest – pollution and climate change does not recognise political boundaries; we cannot insulate ourselves indefinitely from our actions.

Markets and neo-liberals

The concept of the 'market' is fundamental to neo-liberal economics that underpins the policies of the WTO and its powerful Northern members. Neo-liberal economists argue that if their policies were implemented in full – without the subsidies and restrictions which benefit some countries – the market will be able to operate effectively, only then will everyone, rich and poor, North and South, benefit from the market. They believe that the theory is right, only the implementation is flawed.

The importance of the market is the enduring influence of the 'classical' economists of the 18th and 19th Centuries who are still held in high regard by today's policy makers. A leading figure was the Scot, Adam Smith (1723-1790), who in *The Wealth of*

Nations (1776) set out his belief that individualistic, self-seeking behaviour by consumers and producers will be guided by the 'invisible hand' of market forces to achieve the highest level of welfare for society as a whole. For markets to work in this ideal fashion, several assumptions have to be made. Markets must be perfectly competitive with large numbers of buyers and sellers; consumers must have 'perfect information' about the prices and characteristics of the goods and services on offer; and the price mechanism must capture all the costs and benefits.

It's immediately apparent that not one of these assumptions is met in most markets. In many markets a small number of large companies dominate the market – certainly at the national level, and often internationally as well – British food retailing, and international pharmaceuticals are prime examples. Despite the rise of web sites which compare the prices of consumer goods, in most transactions consumers do not have perfect information about the costs and characteristics of competing products. The final assumption, that all the costs and benefits of a product or service are included in the price is also flawed.

Prices rarely reflect the full cost of a product. The pursuit of profit has almost always been at the expense of the environment and people. Mining for raw materials has poisoned rivers, over-harvesting of renewable resources has wiped out species, pollution from processing and disposal of waste has devastated eco-systems. Bad working conditions have caused horrifying occupational diseases and pollution has destroyed communities. And the social costs follow – loss of livelihoods and increased health needs. These costs are met by society as a whole, reflected in reduced quality of life or in the real costs of cleaning up the oil spills or paying disability benefits to sufferers. Who is paying for the healthcare of the victims in Bhopal? Not Dow Chemical, who bought Union Carbide following the disaster and who are now disclaiming any responsibility for the survivors.

Of course many companies do try to be responsible and believe that improving working conditions and reducing environmental impact will bring them business benefits. Fairtrade importers explicitly include additional costs to pay a higher price to producers, to provide, for example, healthcare and education. Modern environmental legislation rests on the 'polluter pays' principle – in theory at least – that companies should 'internalise' the costs of pollution; they, and not society, should pay these costs.

Many people are prepared to pay a premium for products which have higher than normal environmental and/or social standards – the boom in organic food and fairtrade products is proof of this. But why should we have to pay more for products which do not damage the environment, which do not exploit people? Why should we pay more for a product made out of recycled material – which is reducing waste and reducing the use of raw materials? Why should responsible companies see their markets taken away by competitors who undercut them purely by driving down standards, by cutting corners, by polluting land, water and air, by harming workers and local communities?

For a market to allocate scare resources effectively, the true costs of production, including environmental and social costs, must be included in the price. Without this, a sustainable economy is pie in the sky. Indeed many economists now argue that the way forward for a sustainable economy is to incorporate environmental and social cost into prices. This can be done using various economic instruments such as taxes, charges and tradable permits. The Royal Commission on Environmental Pollution[6] for example, argues that the impact of aircraft on climate change should be accounted for by imposing take-off and landing 'climate protection charges' to increase the price of air travel to reflect the cost to the environment – and hence remove the unfair subsidy air travel enjoys through tax free fuel.

Despite the flawed assumptions on which it rests, the market is, for many goods and services, probably the most effective way of allocating resources. What we need to recognise however, are two significant limitations of the market. Firstly, legislation is required to take account of the flawed assumptions – anti-monopoly legislation is one example. Secondly, while many social and environmental costs can and should be incorporated into prices, this approach has its limits. Some economic theorists allocate costs to things like a sick child or a species driven to extinction. We must recognise – and policy makers must accept – that some things don't belong in the market. Many of the economic and social problems facing us need to be seen for what they are – issues that need decisions based on ethical and moral values. Allocating costs to them and pretending the market will solve the problem is an abdication of responsibility.

Since the 1980s the market has encroached ever deeper into all aspects of our lives. To say that political decisions must be based on ethics and morality, now sounds either naïve or heretical. But we have always placed 'value' on things which cannot be given a price in the market. We can value liberty and, through our laws, collectively agree that if someone commits a murder they should be deprived of their liberty – without putting a price on liberty. We can value landscapes, historic buildings and open space and we can protect them through planning law – in principle at least, we are saying that these things are beyond price, they are outside the market. We need to remind ourselves that it is possible to make decisions without putting a price on everything, and we need to develop better, more robust decision-making processes which help us as we have to deal with ever more complex economic, social and environmental conflicts.

What will a sustainable economy actually look like? Who knows – but it must be an economy where the pursuit of profit, at the very least, does not destroy the environment or diminish the life of others. At best, in a sustainable economy, the pursuit of profit will actually enhance the environment and make other people's lives better. In addition, in a sustainable economy we will be taking account of the future as well. This means prices that reflect the true social and environmental costs of production. It means recognising that some matters belong outside the market and are more properly addressed through political and ethical debate. It means trade that respects human rights and democracy, protects the weak from the powerful, and where no one is appropriating more than their fair share of resources.

There is an almost insurmountable barrier to achieving a

sustainable economy in Scotland alone. Current trade patterns are extractive and exploitative – environmentally and socially. Introducing tariffs and regulations which internalise the true costs of production, is not only beyond the powers of the Scottish parliament, it would be in direct contravention of World Trade Organization rules. Contravening WTO rules results in stringent penalties which would cause severe economic difficulties. (Incidentally, the penalties for contravening international human rights and environmental treaties are trivial in comparison.)

Working towards a sustainable economy

In the late 18th Century the slave trade was rife and Britain had a large share of this highly profitable business. Slavery formed the economic basis of the sugar industry in the British West Indies. It was generally recognised as being inevitable, part of 'the natural order', and essential to British commercial interests. In the early 19th Century the mood changed as activists campaigned, first for the abolition of the trade in slaves by British subjects (achieved in 1806), and then for the outright abolition of slavery within the British Empire – resulting in the Slavery Abolition Act of 1833.

The activists, among whom women played a central role, made people aware, not just of the horrors, but also the immorality of slavery. Politicians and public opinion followed their lead. Campaigners were pitting themselves against the establishment – and the 'natural order' of things. (The Bishop of Exeter received £12,700 from the British government in compensation for the loss of his 665 slaves.)

In the same way, activists today, in the North and South, are making visible the exploitation and damage we are causing through our over-consumption and through the trading systems our government endorses. The entrenched interests of the establishment – especially the multinational corporations – might appear insurmountable. The anti-slavery campaigners succeeded. Politicians and civil society must rise to this new challenge, which is just today's version of the same injustice. We must show imagination, courage and leadership and champion a sustainable economy – for Scotland and the world. This agenda has no fundamental conflict with any mainstream political philosophy, it not only commands the moral high ground, it is also entirely pragmatic – our health, our wealth and our security depend on it. A programme for a sustainable economy has two tasks. Firstly, to identify and implement actions within the powers of the Scottish Parliament and the current trade rules, to promote social and environmentally beneficial trade. Secondly, to propose changes and alternatives to these current and proposed WTO rules, which would promote a sustainable economy.

Much of this work is already being carried out by activists and academics across the world. More studies may be necessary, but as a starting point action within current trade rules should include:

- All major companies operating in Scotland should follow international best practice in corporate social responsibility, including publishing externally verified social and environmental reports;
- The Enterprise Networks must recognise the fundamental importance of corporate social responsibility and sustainable development to Scotland's long term success;
- All central and local government departments and agencies must adopt and continually improve enviromentally and socially responsible purchasing policies;
- We must develop more effective decision-making processes – for business and government – which not only address environmental, social and economic issues, but also recognise that there can be value without price;
- The Scottish Parliament's scrutiny of all legislation for its impact on social justice and sustainable development must be greatly enhanced.

In addition there should be action on existing and proposed trade rules[7].

- There must be a proper assessment of the impact of

GATS, independent of the WTO, to look at the social, economic and environmental effects of GATS, not just its effects on trade[8]. No further negotiations on GATS should take place until the results of this assessment are public.

- The WTO system must be reformed to enable poorer countries to participate adequately to influence international trade negotiations. This must include greater internal transparency, and must address the role of the Director General and secretariat staff, which currently seems far from impartial.
- The WTO system must have greater external transparency – there must be opportunities for more informed input and discussion which takes into account the views of wider civil society.
- There must be more effective processes for consultation with other international organisations, such as the Convention on Biological Diversity and the United Nations Human Rights bodies.
- At a national level there must be consultation with all relevant stakeholders, especially those marginalised from policy making.
- There must be additional parliamentary scrutiny of developments at WTO.
- Perhaps most importantly, WTO must not be allowed to overrule Multilateral Environmental Agreements.

The challenge for Scottish politics is to show courage and vision; to see the calls of civil society, not as tiresome challenges to the comfortable status quo, but as opportunities for Scotland to promote its long term interests by championing a better world for people everywhere.

References

[1] *Eight Broken Promises: Why the WTO isn't working for the world's poor*, Oxfam Briefing Paper 9. Oxfam International, 2001.

[2] *Europe's Double Standards: How the EU should reform its trade policies with the developing world*, Oxfam Briefing Paper 22. Oxfam International, 2002.

[3] *Stephen Byers MP takes a stand on trade*, Christian Aid Press release 12/12/02.

[4] *Out of Service: the development dangers of the General Agreement on Trade in Services*, World Development Movement. March 2002.

[5] *From Environmental Space to Ecological Debt – a European Perspective. Martin Rocholl*, Friends of the Earth Europe. November 2001.

[6] *The Environmental Effects of Civil Aircraft in Flight*, Royal Commission on Environmental Pollution. 2002.

[7] The proposals below draw on the Open Letter on Institutional Reforms in the WTO, from International, IATP, ActionAid, FOE International, CIEL, and Oxfam International. October 2001.

[8] The GATS negotiating guidelines, agreed in March 2001, state that an assessment should be carried out, and 'Further negotiations may only commence after conclusions from this first assessment have been drawn'. No assessment has been undertaken, and negotiations are ongoing. The UN Sub-committee on the Promotion of Human Rights has called for a similar assessment. See *Out of Service* op. cit.

7

Mosaic not monolith

A *just transition to a sustainable economy*

RICHARD LEONARD

Obviously we cannot go on protecting dirty industries and need
to move away from a 'toxic economy' to a 'sustainable society'.
(GMB special report to 2001 GMB Congress)

Cooperative economy and participatory democracy

It is a welcome sign of the times that a major trade union like the
GMB can embrace the green agenda. In a Special Report to the
2001 GMB Congress union representatives called for a British
'Just Transition' programme of industrial restructuring. Echoing
the model developed by unions in Canada and the US it called for
a radical shift in the economy under-pinned with redeployment to
sustainable jobs.

Green jobs are often considered as those in the design,
manufacture and application of green technology. These are of
course important, but our objective must be to make every job a
green job. With the right industrial policy framework established
by the Scottish Parliament, Scotland could become the green
enterprise centre of Europe. That requires a new economics. It is
a new economics which challenges the Blairite third way of the
market plus social justice. It is a new economics built on two
pillars: a co-operative economy and a participatory democracy. A
co-operative economy is neither market-led nor a command
economy. A participatory democracy is where people are
entrusted with economic as well as political citizenship, where the
objective is a more egalitarian and democratic society.

The elements in this strategy are more easily realisable in Scotland because of devolution. But with long overdue democratic reform now in the pipeline, other parts of the UK could look to and learn from the Scottish experience.

The sunrise industries are in green technology and in developing restorative production processes. Renewable energy is a good example of this.

Planning ahead for energy

The European Commission estimates that a doubling of energy from renewables from 6% to 12% could create between 500,000 and 800,000 new jobs. Even with George W Bush's stand on the Kyoto agreement on pollution reduction the question is not whether or not these jobs will come, but more where they will be located. Indeed Bush's decision has sparked still greater pressure for a new post-Kyoto consensus to accelerate emission cuts. This has manifested itself in a paradigm-shifting Labour commitment to increase the proportion of Scotland's electricity generated from renewable sources to 40 per cent by 2020.

In Government enterprise-speak there is a lot of talk about high technology and the knowledge economy. But in fact there must be support for intermediate technology, even low technology too. Our goal must be a mosaic not monolith. Here the international experience of wind energy is instructive.

In Denmark the Industry has been based on simple farm based windmill technology. Contrast that with the USA whose industry has been dominated by the aerospace sector. Yet it is the intermediate technology of Denmark which has been the winner. It is Denmark not the USA which is the success story.

The arrival of Danish wind firm Vestas in Campbeltown, Argyll is therefore welcome though not entirely surprising. But it is clear that the UK needs to develop its own wind manufacturing base so that we do not just become a home for overseas owned screwdriver plants.

A sustainable economy will be based on a diverse industrial

structure where local production more closely reflects local need. We need a strategy of import substitution. New jobs can be created by developing new products and by providing goods and services locally which were previously made outside Scotland or the United Kingdom.

That's why changes in Regional Development rules are so important, so that indigenous manufacturers, not just inward investors get a fair share of public investment. For too long renewable technologies have been researched and developed here but put into full production overseas. The most obvious recent example is the case of photovoltaics designed to harness the sun's energy which have been developed by two British companies, Pilkington and BP, but manufactured overseas. This is not a problem unique to the energy sector: research and inventions pioneered at home all too often fail to generate domestic manufacturing employment.

In Scotland we need a vision, which must be championed by the Scottish Parliament, to become the 'green enterprise centre of Europe'. We have ample experience in clean energy technologies. Hydro power is well established. Flu Gas Desulphurisation and low NOx burners have been pioneered by Babcocks in the West of Scotland, Howdens have been involved in renewables and John Brown Engineering in Clydebank have been important suppliers to the Combined Heat and Power market.

The problem is that whilst Babcocks is surviving through diversification into construction and indeed is now bidding for contracts to manufacture wind turbines, Howdens after 100 years no longer manufactures and John Brown Engineering's gates were locked for the last time in March 2001 after 150 Years of history. The lost jobs and wasted skills represent a loss which is social, economic and, potentially, environmental.

There are some smaller embryonic Scottish companies in the field of renewable energy many of which have great potential for growth. Some sectors are stronger than others at the moment. For example Scotland is in a particularly strong position in wave power. We have world-leading wave power experts. We have innovative wave power companies, and significantly considerable maritime engineering expertise thanks to North Sea oil and gas exploration. We are world leaders in design, research, development and construction. We have extensive expertise in electrical, mechanical and hydraulic component design and manufacture and if we look at the optimum locations for wave power the North and West of Scotland comes up time and time again. That's why the Scottish Executive's decision to locate a Scottish Marine Energy Test Centre in Orkney is such an important step forward.

But there must be planning for commercial production now. That will require a Government commitment to open up a UK energy market for wave energy in the next few years. Only by developing a home market will UK firms have any real hope of supplying the burgeoning global market for renewables.

There are also great opportunities for sea-based wind energy. It is against this background that we should think about the continued depression in the oil rig fabrication industry. A breakthrough has been made thanks to public investment at Arnish in the Western Isles, where the Lewis offshore fabrication yard has been re-equipped and refurbished to house a new wind turbine manufacturing facility run by the Welsh-owned Cambrian Engineering.

Yards like this provide manufacturing facilities close to the sea, they contain the skills including research and development capacity. We have a great opportunity to provide socially and environmentally useful work. This work on renewable energy development must form part of a coherent diversification plan which includes the decommissioning of rigs in our oil rig yards.

So we are not just talking about specialist green jobs like environmental consultants but also opportunities for semi-skilled and un-skilled occupations.

If these opportunities are seized there is a compelling case for Scotland's Western Highlands and Islands to be linked by subsea cable to the National Grid. This will require significant investment but weighed against alternatives like big power station construction could prove to be best value.

Restructuring for a stakeholder economy

Let there be no doubt that the market alone will not exploit any of these opportunities. There is a long pipeline of investment in renewables. Spontaneous forces of the market will not work, not least because the electricity market is rigged in favour of nuclear power thanks to the 'must take' clauses of the privatisation agreement. Despite the engineering, design and huge financial difficulties of British Energy this agreement is still likely to be revised, but not removed, in 2005.

There are also barriers arising from the ownership structure of industry in this country. Many of the leading companies are either overseas owned or run from the City of London and driven by short term thinking.

It is important in the wider sense that the Scottish Parliament supports a renaissance in manufacturing. There is terrific export potential. Manufacturing is often at the cutting edge of technology and over a half of service sector jobs are reliant upon manufacturing industry.

Most of the climate change levy to date has funded the 0.3% cut in employers National Insurance Contributions. However, the Chancellor has also ear-marked money from the levy for research and development into renewables, although it is not clear whether this is enough or indeed, whether the emphasis should be less on research and development and more on full production.

Whilst we must go beyond the market, we do not want to repeat the mistakes of the previous half century. Energy policy must be about making the best use of our resources to end fuel poverty and ensure adequate living conditions. Not, as all too often it has been, about building lots of power stations.

It is important that unions, environmentalists, energy companies, manufacturers and government work together. Indeed there will be times when a pincer movement can be especially valuable. With trade unions putting pressure on companies from below and the Scottish Parliament or Westminster putting pressure on from above, policy makers need to speak to trade unionists.

That must include going beyond the full time union officials and speaking to representatives from the shop floor which is a huge untapped reservoir of knowledge.

We need an audit of skills and productive capacity in Scotland including a search of research and expertise in our educational establishments to help assess how Scotland can take advantage of the opportunities there are for renewable energy development and manufacture. This must build on the database of wind power market suppliers already established by Scottish Enterprise's Energy Group. The DTI and the Scottish Executive need to see renewable energy as part of a diversification plan for the oil rig fabrication industry, to make use of existing human and skills resources.

Our job is to convince people that sustainability and renewable energy have something to do with politics. Just like 50 years ago we had to convince people that unemployment had something to do with politics. There are great opportunities, it is important they do not pass us by.

Over 25 years ago the last Labour Government with Tony Benn as Energy Minister in the teeth of great hostility set in train some important and exciting investment into renewables. The incoming Tory Government with Nigel Lawson as Energy Secretary threw much of this to the wolves of the market. It is important that this Labour Government and any future Scottish Executive has the vision and the political will to give renewable energy the support it needs.

Regeneration in the social economy

The Scottish Parliament should set its sights on other areas of growth which buck the market and have the potential to create a strong and sustainable social economy.

For example, as the biggest clothing and textiles union in Britain, the GMB has called for greater inter-company co-operation along the lines of the Modena model in Northern Italy. Here resources area shared amongst the various components of the industry – marketing, training, design and finance. Over the last two decades this has turned around an otherwise declining sector of the regional economy. Because this model has worked successfully for the Italian garment industry the much beleaguered clothing industry in Scotland is an obvious starting point for this inter-firm co-operative approach. But other industries may benefit from its ethos too.

There needs to be new capital investment and the development of a new culture combining value-adding and design functions with firm roots in Scotland. But this will only happen with active public intervention to bring together these new forms of industrial organisation: going beyond clusters to genuinely co-operative networks. Instead of rolling over and believing that decline in traditional industries is inevitable, the Scottish Parliament should look to models like this as a way forward.

One of the pioneers of the co-operative movement, Robert Owen, developed his ideas in Scotland. Why shouldn't priority also be given to support for worker co-operatives to create a new 'Mondragon of the North'.

Mondragon is in the Basque country in Spain where links with the Scottish Parliament are already being established. Since its inception in 1956 its growth has been phenomenal. Today more than 50,000 people work in Mondragon co-operatives, in everything from retailing to banking, and significantly and predominantly in manufacturing.

Employee owned businesses like these are more sustainable than conventional forms of business ownership – and much more democratic. They form part of a social economy which is growing rapidly across Europe. But they require financial and Government support and the involvement of trade unions to nurture and sustain them.

As the European Network for Self Help and Local Development 1997 identified. There are a number of features to organisations in the social economy these include:

• Having a local rather than a regional or national focus;

- Having a clear social, ethical or environmental purpose which is achieved at least in part by engaging in trading and income generation;
- Generally non profit distributing;
- Holding their assets in trust for community benefit;
- Seeking to empower the local community by holding resources under local control.

For the Left the social economy is important. Socialism will not spontaneously erupt. The social economy is part of a process of building support for a socialist way of working and living. How can these changes be brought about in Scotland?

First of all there must be recognition of the importance of the local economy and the need for local policy making. Local authorities should be given greater revenue raising rights together with a broader power of general competence which would allow them to be more proactive in promoting pathways to sustainability.

That is why the introduction in the Local Government Act 2003 of a new local authority power to advance 'well being' appears to be a significant advance, although this has yet to be tested. And there is a lack of local accountability of business, despite their being major users of local government services. The continued setting of Uniform Business Rate by central government is not sustainable. It cannot be right that local government only raises around 15 per cent of its own revenue whilst 85 per cent is set centrally.

In economic development local councils and enterprise bodies should be putting more resources into support for co-operatives and community businesses, into environmental projects rather than site clearance, inward investment and assisting start ups. Local initiatives in Scotland have been pioneering this work for years now through organisations like the Wise Group. The Govan Initiative has recently established a Community Learning Academy as part of a community internet project and is poised to capitalise on the arrival in that part of Glasgow of the new BBC

Scotland headquarters through the development of a local creative industries economy generating employment for local people.

Local authorities themselves should be expanding frontline service provision in socially useful areas like home helps and other caring services. There is no reason why cities could not set their own air pollution standards and targets where these are improvements on national standards.

If the concept of the stakeholder economy is to have any meaning, where better than to wake the sleeping giant which is our pension and insurance funds? Institutional shareholders accounted for 47 per cent of UK ordinary shares (at 31 December 2000) with individuals owning just 16 per cent, with the bulk of the remainder (32 per cent) being overseas owned. Yet at the moment five investment managers control two thirds of all UK pension fund assets.

There are two key questions raised by this. First of all what can be done to make these funds more democratically run and accountable to their policy holders? And secondly, what can be done to use these funds most productively and sustainably?

The present crisis in pensions makes these questions even more compelling. Undoubtedly there has been an over reliance on the casino of the stock market to bring the highest returns. The Stock Exchange relies on gambling and ownership transfer rather than real investment in production to operate and is in need of radical and bold reform.

Institutional investors should be considering a more mixed portfolio including more direct primary investment in businesses. There has been an over-exposure to the risk of stock market short-termism by too many pension fund managers. The operation of pension funds is governed by trust law which requires investment decisions to be made in the best interests of scheme beneficiaries. The interpretation of this by the courts has been very narrow. In an age where ethical investment has assumed greater importance, its time that these rules were changed.

With changes to these rules we could establish a Scottish

Provident Fund, which would be charged with a social and green remit to invest sustainably and socially responsibly. The Fund could assume the management of all existing public sector funded Occupational Pension Schemes in Scotland: most obviously, local authorities, Scottish Parliament, civil service and further and higher education employees funds. The Strathclyde Local Government Pension Fund, the biggest in Britain, alone has over £6 billion in its fund. A Scottish Provident management board could be established comprising 50% employee/union nominees and 50% Scottish Parliament/local government appointees.

This should be accompanied by other reforms like the establishment of a Regional Investment Bank structure across the UK – including a Scottish Investment Bank answerable to the Parliament. The Bank should support alternative production and alternative ownership models. Sustainability should be at the core of all its investment decisions.

One of Labour's most radical – and popular – policies in Scotland has been its programme of land reform, including the abolition of feudalism and the right of communities to buy land when it is up for sale with the aid of a Scottish Land Fund. What goes for land reform should go for industrial reform too. Employees and communities should have a legal right to convert an enterprise into an employee owned or community owned one whenever there is a take-over bid, a proposed transfer of production, when there is asset stripping or where closure is proposed.

A more limited version of this right has existed in Italy since 1985. The Marcora Law not only provides for funding the general promotion and development of co-operatives, but also provides special support for workers facing redundancy. It allows for public investment in a workers co-operative of up to three times the value of the employees investment, up to a maximum limit of three years unemployment benefit. There are claw-back facilities if the enterprise fails, but because it helps solve the undercapitalisation problem faced by many co-ops there is a 90 per cent success rate.

Planned industrial diversification is another area needing

strategic support. In the UK, the Defence Diversification Agency has been the dog which hasn't barked. This was set up to use the post-1989 peace dividend to convert military dependent manufacturing industries to civil production. However, under-resourced, lingering in the shadows of the Ministry of Defence and committed to technology transfer rather than company or community diversification, the agency lacks direction and political control.

A new Scottish Defence Diversification Agency coming under the ambit of the Scottish Executive Enterprise Department should be established. It should have a much broader remit, better resources and the dynamism to be pro-active. It requires leadership too. That is why the partnership model developed by Labour local authority initiatives in this field a decade ago should be introduced nationally, with trade union, defence employer and Scottish Executive involvement in a Scottish Defence Diversification Council to give direction to the initiative.

This in turn may provide a template for a broader conversion agency which encourages and financially supports other parts of our industrial base to convert to more sustainable ways of working and more sustainable products and socially useful services. Scottish industry, from mining to motor manufacture to mobile phones, has stumbled when decisions made elsewhere have pulled the rug from under the workers' feet. Shop stewards know their industries are unsustainable, but no-one asks them how to make the jobs sustainable by planned conversion of the industry they're engaged in. A Sustainable Conversion Agency could bring together trade unions, environmental specialists, community representatives and parliamentarians to guide that 'just transition' to a sustainable economy.

A wide range of unsustainable industries could benefit from such an approach, from North Sea fishing to chemicals from energy to pharmaceuticals. Many of these are currently facing imposed cuts through resource shortages or phasing out products. All require transitional support so that the workers affected are not simply seen as inevitable and acceptable casualties of restructuring, but are given fairness and justice, and can participate in making the transition to new industries and new forms of work.

The Intermediate Technology Institute in Aberdeen aimed at building economic development post-oil shows an existing commitment in this area which should be developed along the lines suggested.

Social policy for economic democracy

It is not just economic policy which can contribute to economic transition. In a joined-up government, social policy should be directed to economic sustainability and vice versa. The Scottish Parliament has responsibility for directing our education system. From the very outset education should encourage values of self reliance and conservation. There is too much talk of education being used to produce human resources for the disposal of business. Education is often linked to Britain's productivity gap. The fact is there is not so much a productivity gap as a production gap – a century old investment gap. It can be no co-incidence that UK workers' productivity is relatively poor when we also work significantly longer hours than anywhere else in Europe. New investment initiatives and a shorter working week would be better ways of starting to plug this productivity gap.

The opportunities afforded by education and training at all ages should not be missed. The Scottish Executive's Lifelong Learning Strategy (February 2003) recognises the role of education in achieving sustainable development. As Agenda 21 made clear, people in their workplaces and their communities are at the heart of the transition to sustainability. They should have the opportunity to learn not just the skills of the next job, but to contribute to what kind of jobs they and their children will have.

Scotland's universities could link up better with local communities and local businesses to produce more socially useful research and development. The wealth of educational, research and development knowledge of the higher education sector is being increasingly turned into a commodity in the open market. At the same time, community groups struggle to access the kinds of expertise which would help them to tackle the economic and social problems which they experience first hand. The Scottish Executive has shown its willingness to depart from Westminster on student fees, and could lead the way in promoting academic accountability.

The glue that will hold this alternative economic and social model together will be democracy. Democracy must not stop in Edinburgh. There must be a democratic shift from the centre to local government and for popular control over pension funds for new ownership structures for industry including greater employee ownership.

It will mean a more participatory democracy where citizens take back power delegated by politicians and bureaucrats to business leaders and pension fund managers.

There is a real need for a new left strategy in Scotland. One which makes socialism and sustainability the language of common sense, which shows there are collectivist alternatives and that these are the most effective way of building the just transition to the sustainable Scottish economy that we need.

8

A Toolkit for Activists

What can bring about the sustainable economy?

MARY SPOWART

How can the kinds of changes needed for a sustainable economy in Scotland be achieved? Many of the issues raised in the chapters of this book are matters of policy emphasis and practice which can be influenced within civic society and through the work of NGOs, trades unions and economic and educational organisations. Other issues require Scottish, Westminster or European legislation which need focused lobbying and campaigns. Moreover, the separation between these categories is not clear cut. The devolution settlement is not fixed and there is a degree of latitude whereby further powers could be devolved to the Scottish Executive were that to be agreed by both Parliaments. There are spending commitments inherent in many of the suggestions. However, the Scottish Executive's underspend in 2001-2 was £643 million. It would seem therefore that initial funding for these initiatives is not an insurmountable problem. It is somewhat difficult to understand why, when sustainable development appears to be a buzz word of the Scottish Executive that this underspend occurred and the monies were not spent on policy initiatives that truly delivered an economy that is sustainable.

The issues raised also have varying opportunities to proceed: some needing civic campaigning; others policy reform; some legislative change and yet others all three. A more detailed analysis of the policy changes needed, and the opportunities which this provides for activists or anyone interested in Scotland's future can be found at www.newpolitics.org.uk.

Summary of policy changes

The tables below list a selection of the policy issues raised by the authors, along with the action required to make the changes. They are ranked in groups according to how achievable they seem to be in the current political climate.

A. In these areas of policy change, there is already commitment from the authority responsible. The main action needed is encouragement for policy to be improved, implemented or enacted.

Issues (with chapter in which it is raised, by author's initials)	Action Required
Establish a Scottish Renewables Community Initiatives fund and targets. (SB)	Scottish Executive Primary Legislation needed. Civil Society can promote policy shift
Stimulate renewable energy generation. Diversify oil fabrication yards and other areas of industrial decline, into renewable energy generator production. (RL)	Scottish Exec policy shift needed. Civil society should lobby.
End fuel poverty. (RL)	Scottish Exec policy already, although civil society pressure needed for mechanisms and implementation, including by local authorities.
Promote bus services, home zones, traffic calming, planning new developments. (SB)	In place. Civil society can promote.

B. In these areas of policy change, there is already some commitment from the authorities responsible. Rather more pressure is needed from civil society to ensure that policy is meaningful.

Issues	Action Required
Ensure that Strategic Environmental Assessment embeds environmental criteria into decision making. (SB)	Elements already in Scottish Exec policy but well short of embedding. Scottish Exec Primary Legislation required by EU directive. Civil society pressure needed to ensure strong policy and implementation.
Promote social and environmental responsibility in business. (OL)	Policy change from Exec with pressure from Civil society. Civic Scotland can promote voluntary mechanisms. Change to companies law at Westminster also useful.
Establish a Scottish Defence Diversification Agency within the Enterprise Department. (RL)	Policy change from Exec with pressure from civil society.

C. The issue is not entirely opposed by the current policy direction. Persuasion will be necessary for it to be acted on.

Issues	Action Required
Appoint a dedicated environment minister. (SB)	Scottish Exec policy shift with civil society pressure.
Promotion of organics. (SB)	Civil society action is growing. Scottish Exec Primary Legislation would help.
Community participation in economic and civil society. (3B)	Civil society action encouraged by Scottish Exec.
Reduce light pollution. (BMacL)	Scottish Exec policy shift with civil society pressure.
Establish a Sustainable Conversion Agency. (RL)	Scottish Exec policy shift with civil society pressure.

SCOTLANDS OF THE FUTURE

D. The issue is contentious, with some opposition but some potential sympathy. It may be achievable through focussed campaigning and lobbying.

Issues	Action Required
Energy efficiency to be considered in major investment in new and replacement schools. (SB)	Significant Scottish Exec policy shift. Civil society campaigning needed at policy level and with individual investments.
Increase understanding and commitment to social enterprise in Executive, Enterprise Agencies and business. (MB)	Scottish Exec policy shift needed. Civil society can put pressure on to Executive and Agencies, and can raise awareness directly.
Local Authorities to have greater powers of general competence and revenue raising powers. (RL)	Scottish Exec Primary Legislation needed. Campaign from civil society.

E. The issue is not popular. A lot of work will be necessary to build up the initiative for changes in the future.

Issues	Action Required
Infrastructure and regulatory changes to encourage social enterprise. (MB)	Scottish Exec policy shift needed, civil society can pressurise.
Local Government Finance from Land Value Taxation. (MB)	Scottish Exec policy shift and Primary Legislation needed. concerted campaign in civil society.
Promotion of equality in 'Family friendly' working conditions. (BMacL)	A culture change is needed. Civil society can campaign and also promote in own employment practices, collective bargaining etc.
Planning reform. (SB)	Scottish Exec policy shift and Primary Legislation – concerted campaign in civil society needed.

F. The issue is very unpopular and is opposed by the responsible agent. It is unlikely much headway will be made and pressure will be needed to bring issue into dialogue.

Issues	Action Required
Develop domestic renewable energy Market. (RL & SB)	Policy change and primary legislation needed at Westminster and the Scottish Executive. Campaigning and practical initiatives from civil society.
Regional development and structural fund changes. (RL)	EU Policy shift and legislation, Westminster policy shift and Primary Legislation, Scottish Exec policy shift and Primary Legislation. Campaigning in civil society.
More active management of the power grid. (SB)	Westminster policy change Scottish Exec policy change and Primary Legislation. Campaigning in civil society.
Redistribution through reform of Income Taxes. Abolish exemptions from VAT and stamp duty (BMacL), or abolish VAT and stamp duty. (MB)	Policy change and Primary Legislation at Westminster and Scottish Executive. Campaigning in civil society.
Introduce Basic Income scheme. (MB)	Policy change and Primary Legislation at Westminster and Scottish Executive. Campaigning in civil society.
Changes in banking practice to promote community investment. (BMacL)	Campaigning and awareness raising in civil society. Possibility of Community Reinvestment Act in Westminster.

G. The issue involves considerable change and is very unpopular. It is opposed by the agency responsible who is virtually immune from the democratic process.

Long term tactical alliance building and extreme pressure will be needed.

Issues	Action Required
Trust laws changed to democratise pension funds. (RL)	Policy change and Primary Legislation at Westminster and Scottish Executive. Campaigning in civil society.
Scottish Investment Bank as part of regional investment banking. (RL)	Scottish Executive could initiate, through civil society campaign. Policy change and Primary Legislation at Westminster needed for structural reform.
Support establishement of co-operatives, including workplace right to buy. (RL)	Policy change and Primary Legislation at Westminster and Scottish Executive. Campaign in civil society.
Change World Trade rules. (OL)	Some influence via Westminster; international civil society likely to be more effective.

Some other books published by **LUATH** PRESS

Eurovision or American Dream? Britain, the Euro and the Future of Europe
David Purdy
ISBN 1 84282 036 2 PB £3.99

Should Britain join the euro?

Where is the European Union going?

Must America rule the world?

Eurovision or American Dream? assesses New Labour's prevarications over the euro and the EU's deliberations about its future against the background of transatlantic discord. Highlighting the contrasts between European social capitalism and American free market individualism, David Purdy shows how Old Europe's welfare states can be renewed in the age of the global market. This, he argues, is essential if European governments are to reconnect with their citizens and revive enthusiasm for the European project. It would also enable the EU to challenge US hegemony, not by transforming itself into a rival superpower, but by championing an alternative model of social development and changing the rules of the global game.

'In this timely and important book David Purdy explains why joining the euro is not just a question of economics, but a question about the future political direction of Britain and its place in Europe.'

PROFESSOR ANDREW GAMBLE, Director: Political Economy Research Centre, Department of Politics, University of Sheffield.

Scotland – Land and Power the agenda for land reform
Andy Wightman
Foreword by Lesley Riddoch
ISBN 0 946487 70 7 PBK £5.00

What is land reform?

Why is it needed?

Will the Scottish Parliament really make a difference?

Scotland – Land and Power argues passionately that nothing less than a radical, comprehensive programme of land reform can make the difference that is needed. Now is no time for palliative solutions which treat the symptoms and not the causes.

Scotland – Land and Power is a controversial and provocative book that clarifies the complexities of landownership in Scotland. Andy Wightman explodes the myth that land issues are relevant only to the far flung fringes of rural Scotland, and questions mainstream political commitment to land reform. He presents his own far-reaching programme for change and a pragmatic, inspiring vision of how Scotland can move from outmoded, unjust power structures towards a more equitable landowning democracy.

'Writers like Andy Wightman are determined to make sure that the hurt of the last century is not compounded by a rushed solution in the next. This accessible, comprehensive but passionately argued book is quite simply essential reading and perfectly timed – here's hoping Scotland's legislators agree.
LESLEY RIDDOCH

Luath Press Limited
committed to publishing well written books worth reading

LUATH PRESS takes its name from Robert Burns, whose little collie
Luath (*Gael.*, swift or nimble) tripped up Jean Armour at a wedding and gave
him the chance to speak to the woman who was to be his wife and
the abiding love of his life. Burns called one of *The Twa
Dogs* Luath after Cuchullin's hunting dog in *Ossian's
Fingal.* Luath Press was established in 1981 in the
heart of Burns country, and is now based a few
steps up the road from Burns' first lodgings on
Edinburgh's Royal Mile.
Luath offers you distinctive writing with a hint
of unexpected pleasures.

Most bookshops either carry our books in stock or
can order them for you. To order direct from us,
please send a £sterling cheque, postal order, international money order or your credit card details (number,
address of cardholder and expiry date) to us at the address
below. Please add post and packing as follows: UK – £1.00
per delivery address; overseas surface mail – £2.50 per delivery address; overseas airmail – £3.50 for the first book to each delivery
address, plus £1.00 for each additional book by airmail to the same address.
If your order is a gift, we will happily enclose your card or message at no
extra charge.

Luath Press Limited
543/2 Castlehill
The Royal Mile
Edinburgh EH1 2ND
Scotland
Telephone: 0131 225 4326 (24 hours)
Fax: 0131 225 4324
email: gavin.macdougall@luath.co.uk
Website: www.luath.co.uk